A Taste of the Outer Banks

A Taste of the Outer Banks

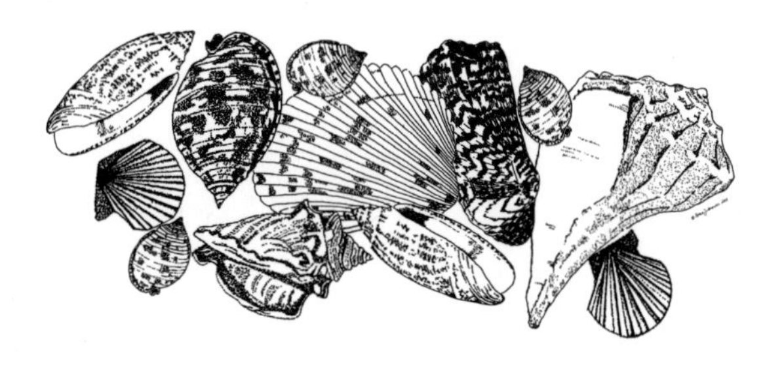

Loren Fedorowicz

2015

Printed in the United States of America.

ISBN: 1-59098-768-3

FOURTH EDITION

www.ohiorivertradingcompany.com

For Kevin,
Felicia and Chet,
Shari and the *RELEASE*

Thank you …

Sections

APPETIZERS

The Currituck Lighthouse, one of the many lighthouses along North Carolina's Outer Banks was once used as a navigational aid to warn mariners of the dangerous Diamond Shoals. Built in 1875, the Currituck Lighthouse is 163 feet tall and contains over 200 steps to the top. Unlike the other decorated lighthouses along the Outer Banks, this tower is very recognizable because its nearly one million bricks have remained unpainted. The Currituck Lighthouse is still in service today with its original first-order Fresnel lens.

FRENCH BREAD TOPPING

1 quart mayonnaise
2 cups cheddar cheese, grated
3 cloves garlic, finely chopped
1 bunch fresh parsley, finely chopped
2 cups grated Parmesan cheese
6 green onions, diced
1 Loaf of Italian or French bread (cut horizontally through the middle)

Preheat oven to 400° F. Combine all of the ingredients and spread 1/3 of the mixture on both cut halves of the entire length of the bread. Place on baking sheet, uncovered. Bake at 400° F for 10 minutes. This recipe makes enough to cover 6 halves of bread. This cheese spread will keep in the refrigerator for a week.

FRIED TOMATOES

Select firm, slightly under ripe tomatoes and cut 1/4" thick slices. Season with salt and pepper; dredge in flour. Melt butter in a frying pan and cook until lightly browned.

HARBOR ISLAND SEAFOOD COCKTAIL

1 pound cooked flaked crab meat, whole shrimp, oysters, or flaked fish
1/2 cup celery, chopped (optional)
1 cup bottled chili sauce
1 T. fresh lemon juice
1 tsp. horseradish
1/2 tsp. onion, grated
Splash of Tabasco
Lemon wedges

Combine chili sauce, lemon juice, horseradish, onion and Tabasco sauce. Place seafood in cocktail cups; spoon sauce over seafood mixture. Garnish with chopped celery, if desired. Serve with lemon wedges and bread sticks or crackers. Serves 6.

CRABMEAT COCKTAIL

1/2 pound cooked crab meat, flaked
1/2 cup celery, finely chopped
6 T. catsup
2 T. fresh lemon juice
1 T. horseradish
1/2 tsp. onion, grated
1 tsp. Worcestershire
Splash of Tabasco
Salt to taste
Lettuce for garnish

Combine crab meat and celery and place in lettuce-lined cocktail cups. Cover with plastic wrap and chill. Combine remaining ingredients and spoon over crab meat mixture before serving. Serve with breadsticks or crackers. Serves 2.

NORTH ATLANTIC CRAB MEAT COCKTAIL

1 pound cooked crab meat, flaked
1 cup celery, chopped
3/4 cup bottled chili sauce
1/4 cup lemon juice
1-1/2 T. horseradish
1 T. Worcestershire
1/4 tsp. onion, grated
1/2 tsp. salt
Splash of Tabasco
Lettuce for garnish

Gently toss crab meat and celery together. Place in individual lettuce-lined cocktail cups, cover with plastic wrap and chill. Combine remaining ingredients and chill until ready to serve. Spoon the sauce over the crab meat mixture before serving. Serve very cold. Serves 4.

OYSTER COCKTAIL

1-1/2 pints raw oysters, drained
1 cup catsup or chili sauce
2 T. wine vinegar
1 T. horseradish
1 T. celery, minced
1 T. onion, minced
1/2 tsp. salt
1 tsp. Worcestershire
Splash of Tabasco
Lettuce
Lemon wedges

Divide oysters into lettuce-lined cocktail cups (about 6 oysters per serving) cover with plastic wrap and chill. Combine remaining ingredients, spoon sauce over oysters immediately before serving. Serves 6.

OYSTER COCKTAIL IN A TOMATO CUP

1 small ripe tomato
4 small raw oysters
1 tsp. horseradish
1 T. lemon juice
1 tsp. cider vinegar
1 tsp. Worcestershire
Splash of Tabasco
Salt, pepper and paprika to taste.

Scald, peel and chill tomato. Carefully hollow out the tomato; finely chop the pulp. Combine tomato pulp with remaining ingredients and refrigerate. To serve, place the oysters into the tomato. Spoon the sauce over oysters in the tomato. Chill until ready to serve. Serves 1.

OREGON INLET OYSTER COCKTAIL

12 small raw oysters
2 T. fresh lemon juice
Pinch of salt
Dash of paprika
2 T. catsup
1 tsp. horseradish
Splash of Tabasco

Remove oysters from shells; set aside. Combine remaining ingredients and pour over chilled oysters. Eat immediately or chill until ready to serve. Can be served in cocktail cups or in cleaned and dried oyster shells. Serves 2.

CRABMEAT DIP

3 oz. pkg. cream cheese, softened
1/2 cup mayonnaise
2/3 cup tomato soup, undiluted
1/2 pound crab meat, cooked
1 clove garlic, minced
Dash of salt
Dash of pepper
Tabasco (optional)

Stir in mayonnaise and tomato soup into softened cream cheese and blend well. Mix in crabmeat, garlic, salt, pepper and Tabasco. Serve with crackers, vegetables or chips.

BAKED CRABMEAT DIP

8 oz. pkg. cream cheese, softened
2 T. onion, chopped
1 T. milk
1 tsp. horseradish
1/4 tsp. salt
1/4 tsp. pepper
1/2 pound crabmeat, cooked

Preheat oven to 375° F. Mix all ingredients and place in greased baking dish. Bake for 15 minutes. Serve hot with crackers or vegetables.

CAPE FEAR CLAM AND CHEESE DIP

8 oz. pkg. cream cheese, softened
4 oz. blue cheese, crumbled
1/3 cup minced clams, drained
1 T. chives or green onion, finely chopped
1/4 tsp. salt
Tabasco

Combine all ingredients and chill. Serve with crackers or chips.

SHARI'S SHRIMP DIP

8 oz. pkg. cream cheese, softened
1 can cream of shrimp soup
1 small can tiny shrimp
Garlic powder to taste

Blend all ingredients in a food processor and chill. Enjoy with crackers or vegetables.

JUDY ANNE'S CLAM DIP

2 – 8 oz. pkgs. cream cheese, softened
1 can minced clams, drained
2 tsp.onion, grated
Dash of garlic salt
Dash of Paprika

Drain clams; reserve liquid. Mix clams and cream cheese together; mix in onions and garlic salt. Add as much clam liquid as needed for desired dipping consistency. Sprinkle with paprika for garnish. Enjoy with crackers, chips or vegetables.

HOT CRAB DIP

1 pound extra sharp cheddar cheese, shredded
2 cans crabmeat
2 cans cream of shrimp soup
1/4 tsp. garlic salt
1/4 tsp. onion salt
Shake of Tabasco sauce
1/3 cup brandy
1 cup Parmesan cheese

Mix all ingredients in a heavy saucepan over low heat until cheese is melted and the mixture is heated through. Stir frequently to prevent sticking. If too thin, add cornstarch, a little at a time to achieve desired consistency. Serve with favorite chips or crackers.

MY FAVORITE CRAB DIP

1 can crab meat
1-14 oz. can plain artichoke hearts, drained and chopped
1/3 cup onion, chopped
8 oz. pkg. cream cheese, softened
1 cup mayonnaise
3/4 cup parmesan cheese, grated

Preheat over to 350° F. Mix cream cheese and mayonnaise together in a large mixing bowl until well blended. Add onion, crab meat, artichokes, and parmesan cheese; mix well. Place mixture in an oven-proof baking dish. Bake for 15–18 minutes until hot and bubbly but not brown. Serve with a variety of crackers.

HATTERAS ISLAND HOT CLAM DIP

2 - 8oz. pkgs. cream cheese, room temperature
2 cans minced clams, drained - save some juice
2 T. Worcestershire
2 tsp. fresh lemon juice
5 green onions finely chopped
Parsley finely chopped
Red pepper to taste

Combine all ingredients and heat until cheese is melted. Add clam juice, a little at a time, if the dip is too thick. Sprinkle with red pepper and garnish with parsley. Serve hot with favorite crackers.

CRAB PUFFS

2 egg whites, beaten stiff
1 cup mayonnaise
2 cans crab meat
Salt and pepper to taste
Bread
Butter
Paprika

Butter slices of bread on one side; brown under broiler. Mix ingredients together and spread on other side of bread. Sprinkle with paprika and broil until browned.

ROASTED GARLIC

6 heads of garlic
2-1/2 T. olive oil

Preheat oven to 375° F. Spray small baking dish with nonstick cooking spray. Cut approximately 1/4 inch off of the top of garlic bulb and place in dish. Drizzle top of the bulbs with olive oil. Bake for 1 hour, or until garlic is soft. Remove from oven and allow to cool for 10 minutes. Squeeze bulb to extract pulp and spread on favorite toasted bread.

FIESTA DIP

2-15 oz. cans refried beans
4 oz. can chopped green chilies, undrained
1 pint sour cream
1 pkg taco seasoning mix
3 ripe avocados, pitted and peeled
2 T. fresh lime juice
1/2 tsp.salt
Sprinkle of garlic salt
Cheddar cheese, shredded
Tomatoes, chopped
Green onions, sliced
Olives, sliced
Lettuce, shredded

In small bowl, combine refried beans and chilies. Spread on large serving plate. Combine sour cream and taco seasoning and spread evenly over bean mixture. In separate bowl, mash avocadoes, stir in lime juice, salt and garlic salt and spoon evenly over sour cream mixture. Cover; chill for several hours. Before serving, garnish with cheese, tomato, green onions, olives and lettuce. Serve with tortilla chips.

BATTERS, SAUCES, & MARINADES

Situated on Bodie Island near the Roanoke Sound, the Bodie Island Lighthouse, part of the Cape Hatteras National Seashore, was built in 1872. The current tower is actually the third Bodie Island Lighthouse because the first tower collapsed due to poor construction and the second tower was destroyed by Confederate troops. The Bodie Island Lighthouse is 156 feet tall and is still in service today with its original first-order Fresnel lens.

BEER BATTER FISH I

Oil for frying

2 cups flour
1/2 tsp. baking soda
1/2 tsp. baking powder
1 tsp. paprika
1 egg
1 can of beer

Combine all ingredients and mix thoroughly into a batter. Coat fish in batter and fry in hot oil until golden brown.

BEER BATTER FISH II

Oil for frying

1 cup pancake mix
1 cup cracker crumbs
1 can of beer
1 tsp. sugar
2 eggs

Mix ingredients thoroughly and chill for 30 minutes before using. Coat fish in batter and fry in hot oil until golden brown.

GRANDMA'S FISH BATTER

Flour for dredging fish
Oil for frying

1 cup buttermilk

1 lemon, sliced
2 cups pancake mix
2-1/2 cups club soda

Cover fish with buttermilk and lemon and refrigerate for 2 hours. Remove fish from buttermilk, throw away the lemons and dredge fish in flour. Combine club soda and pancake mix to create batter. Dip fish in batter and fry for 4 minutes on each side or until golden brown.

TEMPURA BATTER FOR FISH

Oil for frying
1/2 cup flour
1/2 cup cornstarch
1 tsp. baking powder
1 tsp. baking soda

1 tsp. sugar
1/2 tsp. salt
2/3 cup ice water
1 egg, beaten

Sift dry ingredients together. In a separate bowl, beat egg and water together; combine with dry ingredients. Coat fish in batter and fry in hot oil until golden brown.

SOUTHERN FISH FRY BATTER

Oil for frying

1 cup flour
1 T. baking powder
1/2 tsp. salt
1 tsp. paprika
1 egg
Beer

Sift the dry ingredients together. In a separate bowl, beat egg and 1/2 bottle of beer together; combine with dry ingredients. Mix thoroughly. Coat fish in batter and fry in hot oil until golden brown.

FISH FRY FRIDAY

Oil for frying

1 cup beer
1 cup flour
1/2 tsp. salt

Mix beer and flour and salt together in a bowl, add less flour if thinner batter is desired. Let batter sit for 10 minutes. Dip fish in batter and fry in hot oil until golden brown. Makes 2 cups.

This batter is also good for chicken, or raw vegetables.

BLUFF POINT BEER BATTER

Oil for frying

1 cup of pancake mix
1 cup of beer

Mix beer and pancake mix together in a bowl. Dip fish in batter and fry in hot oil until golden brown. Makes 2 cups.

This batter is also good for chicken or raw vegetables.

CUCUMBER BUTTER FOR FISH

1 medium cucumber
1/2 cup butter

2 tsp. fresh lemon juice
Salt and pepper to taste

Peel and seed cucumber. Grate cucumber; squeeze juice out of pulp and set aside. In a separate bowl, beat remaining ingredients until light and fluffy. Add cucumber pulp; blend thoroughly. Refrigerate until ready to use. This sauce melts when placed on hot fish. Makes 1 cup.

SIMPLE BUTTER SAUCE

1 cup butter
1-1/2 T. fresh lemon juice
Dash of Tabasco
1/2 T. Worcestershire

Melt butter over low heat. Stir in remaining ingredients. Pour over cooked fish or seafood.

Variation:
Add 1/4 cup slivered or sliced almonds to butter and brown lightly before adding remaining ingredients.

HERB SAUCE FOR FISH

1/4 cup butter
3 T. white wine
1 T. fresh parsley, minced
1/2 tsp. salt
2 T. chives, minced
1 tsp. fresh dill, minced

Melt butter in a small saucepan. Mix remaining ingredients together and add to saucepan. Cook over a low heat until thoroughly heated. Pour hot mixture over favorite cooked fish.

LEMON BUTTER SAUCE

1/2 cup butter, melted
2 T. lemon juice
1 tsp. fresh lemon zest
1/4 tsp. salt

Melt butter. Blend all ingredients in small bowl. Makes 1/2 cup.

Serve over fish or steamed vegetables.

Variation:
Add 1/4 cup chopped parsley to the Lemon Butter.

OUT-TO-SEA SAUCE

1 T. butter
1 T. flour
3 T. water
1 tsp. vinegar
2 T. bottled chili sauce
1 T. pimiento, chopped
1/8 tsp. celery seed
1/2 tsp. onion, minced
3 T. mayonnaise

Melt butter in saucepan. Stir in flour; cook over low heat until lightly browned. Stir in all remaining ingredients except mayonnaise. Cook until thickened, stirring constantly. Remove from heat; blend in mayonnaise. Makes 1 cup.

WHITE SAUCE

3 T. butter
3 T. flour
1 cup milk
1/2 tsp. salt
1/8 tsp. white pepper
Favorite herbs and spices (optional)

Melt butter in heavy saucepan. Over medium heat, whisk in flour and cook, stirring constantly for 2 minutes, or until mixture (known as a roux) turns light and airy and begins to bubble. Turn down heat; slowly add the milk, stirring constantly to prevent lumps. Sauce will be thickened and smooth in about 1 minute. Add salt and pepper and cook over low heat for 10 minutes, stirring occasionally. Add favorite seasonings.

Variation:
Cheese Sauce: Add 1/2 cup grated sharp Cheddar cheese to 1 cup White Sauce. Cook, stirring constantly, until cheese is melted. Makes approximately 1 cup.

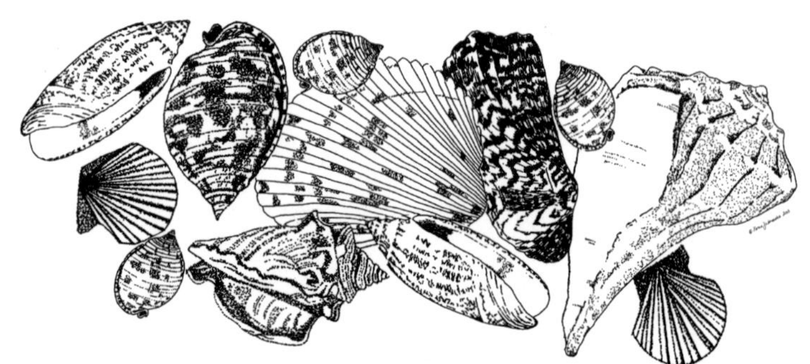

Seashells, found in a variety of beautiful shapes, colors and sizes are actually the outer skeletons of soft-bodied mollusks. Protecting the animal living within, a seashell grows in a slow, continuous fashion beginning the day the animal is born. A seashell and the animal it houses can often reach full maturity within the first two years of its life and depending upon the species can reach a lifespan of thirty years.

CREAM SAUCE

1 cup White Sauce (see WHITE SAUCE recipe on page 20)
1/2 cup heavy cream

Combine ingredients in heavy saucepan. Cook over low heat until hot, stirring occasionally.

Variation:
Herb Cream Sauce: Add 1 tablespoon freshly chopped or 1 teaspoon dried herbs of choice to hot Cream Sauce. Cook over low heat for 3 minutes, stirring occasionally. Make 1-1/2 cups.

KEVIN'S CHEESY SAUCE

1 cup milk
2 cups Cheddar cheese, shredded
1 T. butter
1/2 tsp. salt
1/8 tsp. pepper
1/4 tsp. dry mustard
Dash of cayenne

Mix all ingredients together in a heavy saucepan. Cook over low heat, stirring frequently until cheese is melted. Remove from heat and stir for 1 minute. Serve over fresh vegetables or with chips. Makes 2 cups.

JOCKEYS RIDGE RED CHILI SAUCE

7 oz. can red chili peppers, drained
1/2 cup tomato sauce
1 clove garlic, crushed
1/4 cup olive oil
1-1/2 tsp. salt
1 tsp. oregano
1/4 tsp. cumin

Preheat oven to 400° F. Grease baking sheet. Arrange chilies on baking sheet; bake for 4 minutes. Cool. Rinse chilies in cold water; remove seeds. In bowl, cover chilies with hot water; let stand for 1 hour. Place chilies, with enough water to cover, in a blender or food processor to make a smooth paste. Place chili paste in a saucepan and add enough water to total 3 cups. Gently whisk the water into the paste until well blended. Stir in remaining ingredients; bring to boil. Simmer for 10 minutes, stirring occasionally. Serve with seafood or chicken. Makes 3 cups.

HIGHWAY 12 HOT SAUCE

1 cup whipping cream
2 T. horseradish
2 T. fresh lemon juice
1/8 tsp. salt
1/4 cup parsley, chopped

In mixing bowl, whip cream until stiff. Fold in remaining ingredients. Chill well before serving. Serve with seafood or chicken. Makes 2 cups.

CORE BANKS CREOLE SAUCE

4 slices bacon, diced
2 large onions, chopped
1 cup celery, chopped
2 - 8 oz. cans tomato sauce
2 cups water
4 cloves garlic, crushed
2 tsp. sugar
Salt and pepper to taste
1/4 cup parsley, chopped

Cook bacon in large frying pan or large saucepan for 3 minutes. Add onions and celery; sauté for 5 minutes. Stir in tomato sauce, water, garlic, sugar, salt and pepper. Bring to boil; cover; simmer for 2 to 3 hours. Add parsley just before serving.

WINE SAUCE

1 T. butter
1 cup fresh mushrooms, sliced
1 T. flour
1/2 cup dry red wine
1/4 cup water
Salt and pepper to taste

Melt butter in saucepan; sauté mushrooms over medium heat for 5 minutes. Sprinkle with flour; brown slightly, stirring frequently. Stir in wine and water; cook over medium heat, stirring constantly until thickened. Season with salt and pepper; simmer for 2 minutes. Makes 2 cups.

SHARI'S CLAM SAUCE

3 T. butter
1 T. flour
1/2 tsp. dry mustard
1 cup clam juice
1/4 tsp. salt
1/2 tsp. coarsely ground black pepper

Melt butter in saucepan; blend in flour and mustard. Gradually stir in clam juice; cook over medium heat, stirring constantly, until thickened and smooth. Season with salt and pepper. Serve with steamed clams. Makes 1 cup.

WANCHESE WINE MARINADE

1 cup dry white wine
3 T. vinegar
1/3 cup olive oil
1/3 cup soy sauce
1 T. sugar
1/4 tsp. pepper
1/4 tsp. marjoram
1/4 tsp. basil
1 clove garlic, crushed
1/3 cup favorite barbecue sauce
1 tsp. salt
1/2 tsp. oregano

Place fish in a glass baking dish or a resealable plastic bag. Combine all ingredients. Pour over fish and marinate in the refrigerator for at least 2 hours before cooking. Makes 2-1/2 cups.

ORIENTAL 1969 MARINADE

2 cloves garlic, crushed
1/2 cup soy sauce
1 T. cooking oil
1/2 tsp. salt
1/2 tsp. pepper
1/4 tsp. ginger

Place fish in a glass baking dish or a resealable plastic bag. Combine all ingredients. Pour over fish and marinate in the refrigerator for 30 minutes before cooking. Makes 1/2 cups.

SOUPS
CHOWDERS
STEWS

Built in 1870, the Cape Hatteras Lighthouse was originally designed to warn mariners of the dangerous Diamond Shoals. Now guarding the "Graveyard of the Atlantic," the shipwreck laden waters off the Outer Banks, the Cape Hatteras Lighthouse is the tallest brick lighthouse in the United States. The black and white spiral-striped lighthouse is 210 feet tall and is equipped with a revolving beacon that can be seen for twenty miles. Threatened by erosion, the Cape Hatteras Lighthouse was moved in 1999 from its original location 2900 feet to the southwest for preservation.

QUEEN ANNE'S REVENGE FISH CHOWDER

1 pound of favorite fresh fish
1/2 cup celery, chopped
1/2 cup onion, chopped
1/2 cup carrots, chopped
1 clove garlic, minced
1/2 cup flour
1 quart chicken stock
2 cups potatoes, diced
2 cups cream
3 T. parsley, chopped
4 slices of bacon

Fry bacon in large saucepan until crisp. Drain bacon on paper toweling. Discard all but 2-3 tablespoons of bacon drippings. Crumble bacon and return to pan. Add celery, onion, carrots, garlic and sauté for 5 to 6 minutes or until onion is transparent. Add flour; stir until well mixed. Slowly add chicken stock and potatoes. Cook for 15 minutes or until the potatoes are tender; add bite-size pieces of fish. Cover and cook for an additional 15 minutes or until fish is cooked. Slowly add cream and parsley. Cook over low heat stirring occasionally until thoroughly heated. Serves 4.

OYSTER SOUP

1 quart freshly shucked oysters with liquid
1 large onion, thinly sliced
3 large cloves garlic, minced
2 sticks butter
1-1/2 quarts cold water
3 T. flour
1 tsp. thyme
3 bay leaves
1 cup warm milk
1 cup warm cream
4 T. fresh parsley, finely chopped
Salt and pepper to taste

Melt butter in large saucepan. Sauté onions and garlic until onions are transparent. Stir in flour. Gradually stir in water. Bring to boil, stirring frequently. Lower heat; add seasonings and oysters with liquid. Cover and simmer for 3 hours. Just before serving, add milk and cream. Simmer over a low heat until thoroughly heated. Do not bring to a boil after milk and cream have been added. Boiling will cause the cream to curdle. Garnish with chopped parsley. Serves 6.

OCRACOKE OYSTER STEW

1 quart freshly shucked oysters with liquid
2 cups water
2 tsp. salt
2 T. butter
1/8 tsp. pepper
2 cups milk
1/4 cup cracker crumbs
1 tsp. fresh parsley, chopped

Shuck oysters; reserve liquid. Place only oysters and water in saucepan; bring to a boil. Turn heat to low; cook for 5 minutes or until oysters are plump and edges curl. Remove oysters with a slotted spoon and place in a soup tureen or serving bowl. To the oyster broth add salt, butter and pepper. Heat milk to scalding and add oyster liquid. Strain broth over oysters. Sprinkle with cracker crumbs and chopped parsley. Serves 4.

SHELL CASTLE SHRIMP CHOWDER

2 pounds fresh shrimp
1 cup onions, diced
1 cup celery, diced
1/2 cup green pepper, chopped
1 tsp. garlic, minced
2 T. butter
1 quart water
1 cup potatoes, diced
1/2 cup carrots, sliced
1 can whole kernel corn
1 large can diced tomatoes
2 tsp. salt
1/4 tsp. crushed red pepper flakes

Peel and de-vein shrimp; set aside. In a large kettle melt butter; sauté onions, celery, garlic and green pepper until onions are transparent. Add shrimp, water and remaining ingredients; bring to a boil. Cover and cook until vegetables are tender. Serves 4.

FELICIA'S FRENCH ONION SOUP

4 cups sweet onions, thinly sliced
1 tsp. sugar
1/2 stick butter
2 large cans beef stock
Salt and pepper to taste
Provolone cheese, sliced
French bread or croutons

In a large saucepan, melt butter and sauté onions over a medium low heat until soft. Sprinkle sugar over onions; continue to cook until lightly browned. Add beef stock. Cover; simmer for 1 hour. Check before seasoning with salt. Season with salt if necessary and pepper. When ready to serve, ladle soup into ovenproof soup bowls; place a slice of French bread or croutons on top; cover with cheese. Place the bowls in a preheated broiler, approximately 4" to 5" from heating element until cheese is melted and lightly browned. Serves 8.

STEWED SCALLOPS

1 pound scallops
1 tsp. bottled steak sauce
2 T. butter
3 cups milk
1 cup heavy cream
1 tsp. salt
1/2 tsp paprika
1 T. fresh parsley, chopped

In saucepan combine milk, cream, butter, steak sauce and salt. Heat to scalding over low heat. Add scallops and poach mixture for 5 minutes (do not boil). Ladle into soup bowls. Sprinkle each serving with paprika and parsley. Serves 4.

OAK ISLAND SHRIMP STEW

1 pound fresh shrimp
Cayenne pepper to taste
Salt to taste
1 T. flour
1 T. butter
1 large onion, finely chopped
1 clove garlic, minced
2 cups water
2 T. fresh parsley, chopped

Peel and de-vein; set aside. Season raw shrimp with salt and cayenne pepper. In a medium saucepan, melt butter, add flour and cook until flour is dark brown. Lower heat; add onion and garlic. Cook 5 minutes or until onions are tender. Stir water into mixture a little at a time stirring constantly until well blended. Add shrimp and parsley. Cover; simmer for 45 minutes. Serve over rice. Serves 4.

SUSAN'S SCALLOP STEW

1 pound scallops
1/4 cup butter
1/2 cup sweet onion, chopped
5 medium russet potatoes
2 cups whole milk
2 cups half and half
2 tsp. Worcestershire sauce
1 tsp. salt
1/4 tsp. white pepper
1 T parsley, chopped
Croutons

Peel potatoes and cut into 1" pieces; cook in salted water until tender. Drain; cover to keep warm and set aside. Cut scallops into bite-sized pieces; set aside. Melt butter in a large saucepan; sauté onions until onions are transparent. Add scallops and cook 2-3 minutes or until they become opaque. Add cooked potatoes. Gently stir in milk and half and half. Add Worcestershire sauce, salt and white pepper. Cook over low heat until thoroughly heated. Do not let soup boil as it will curdle. Garnish with parsley and croutons. Serves 4.

CLAM CHOWDER

2 cups chopped, cooked, clams
4 slices bacon, diced
1 cup onion, chopped
4 large potatoes, diced
2 tsp. salt
3 cups milk
2 -12 oz. cans evaporated milk
2 tsp. butter
Salt and pepper to taste

Put diced potatoes in a stock pot with enough water to cover; add 2 teaspoons salt. Bring to boil; reduce heat; simmer until potatoes are tender. Cook bacon in a medium frying pan until crisp. Drain; set aside. Cook onion in bacon drippings until lightly browned. Add to potatoes; simmer for 10 minutes. Add clams, milk and evaporated milk. Heat thoroughly over reduced heat stirring occasionally. Do not boil. Serves 6.

KINNAKEET DILL PICKLE SOUP

8 large russet potatoes
Olive oil
1 medium sweet onion, chopped
1 cup celery, chopped
1/2 cup carrot, shredded (optional)
1-48 oz. can beef stock, plus
1-14 oz. can beef stock
1 – 24 oz. jar deli style dill pickles, any type but sliced
Sour cream
Salt and pepper to taste.

Peel potatoes and cut into bite sized pieces. Place in a stock pot; rinse and drain. Use the beef stock to cook the potatoes; make sure potatoes are covered with beef broth, add the small can of broth if necessary. Bring to a boil; cover and reduce heat. Heat olive oil in a separate pan; sauté onions and celery until onions are lightly browned. Add to potatoes. Continue to cook until potatoes are tender. Meanwhile, drain dill pickles, reserving the juice; grate the pickles and add to potatoes along with the reserved juice. Add carrots if so desired; cook over low heat for 10 minutes. Mash gently into the potatoes to break up pieces if so desired. Taste prior to adding salt. Serve with a dollop of sour cream per bowl. Serves 6.

CEDAR ISLAND CRAB SOUP

1 pound cooked crabmeat
1-1/2 quarts half and half
1 medium onion, diced
2 T. butter
1/2 tsp. white pepper
1/4 cup celery, chopped
Dash of garlic powder
1 T. cornstarch
Salt to taste
Green and/or red pepper for color

In a large sauce pan, sauté onions and celery until onions are transparent. Add remaining ingredients except crab. Cook over low heat, stirring frequently, for approximately 35 minutes or until vegetables are tender. Add crabmeat and cook until thoroughly heated. Serves 4.

SALADS

Ocracoke Lighthouse is the southernmost lighthouse on North Carolina's Outer Banks and is situated on Ocracoke Island. The current lighthouse is 76 feet tall and was originally built in 1823 to provide guidance for the many ships that passed through the very busy Ocracoke Inlet during the 1800s. Ocracoke Lighthouse, with its cemented whitewash exterior is still in operation today with a low-intensity light, making it the oldest active lighthouse in North Carolina.

COROLLA PASTA SEAFOOD SALAD

1 cup cooked crabmeat
1 cup broccoli flowerets
1/2 cup green pepper, diced
1/4 cup green onion, chopped
1/2 cup mayonnaise
2 T. Parmesan cheese
1/2 cup red pepper, diced
1/2 cup water chestnuts, chopped
1 cup cooked pasta of choice
1/4 cup Italian dressing

Gently toss all ingredients together and enjoy. Can be served on a bed of lettuce or plain. Serves 2 to 3.

SHRIMP AND COUSCOUS SALAD

1 cup couscous, uncooked
1-1/2 cups cherry or grape tomatoes
1 cup cooked shrimp
1/4 cup fresh lemon juice
3 T. olive oil
1/4 tsp. pepper
1/2 tsp. salt
Parsley for garnish

Cook couscous according to directions. Combine couscous, tomatoes and shrimp in large bowl and toss gently. Combine lemon juice, olive oil, pepper and salt in separate bowl, whisk together and add to couscous mixture. Serve chilled. Garnish with parsley. Serves 4.

CANDY'S GREEK SALAD

2 cups cherry tomatoes, seeded and cut lengthwise
1 - 6oz. jar green olives, drained
1 - 6oz. can black pitted olives, drained
8 oz. feta cheese, crumbled
1 head of broccoli, cut into bite-sized pieces
1 head of cauliflower, cut into bite-sized pieces

Mix all ingredients together in a large bowl and set aside.

Salad Dressing:
Mix favorite Italian dressing with 1/4 cup red wine vinegar. Pour dressing over salad and toss well. Cover and refrigerate. Allow to marinate for 8 hours.

SPINACH SALAD

1 pound spinach, cleaned and torn into bite-sized pieces
3 green onions, diced
1 unpeeled apple, diced
5 slices bacon
1/3 cup sliced almonds

Fry bacon; drain, cool, crumble, and set aside. Drain all but 1 tablespoon of bacon drippings. Lightly brown almonds in the reserved drippings. Combine all ingredients including bacon and almonds in a large bowl; cover and chill until ready to serve. When ready to serve, pour on Salad Dressing and toss gently.

SALAD DRESSING
1/4 cup olive oil
3T. wine vinegar
1 tsp. sugar
1/2 tsp. mustard
Combine ingredients in tight fitting container and shake well. Mix all ingredients together and refrigerate.

CANDY'S PERFECT CAESAR SALAD

2 heads romaine lettuce, rinsed and dried
1/2 cup oil
1/4 cup fresh lemon juice
2 cloves garlic, chopped
1-1/2 tsp. Worcestershire sauce
1/2 tsp. salt
1/4 tsp. pepper
1 egg, beaten
1/2 cup Parmesan cheese
1 pkg. favorite croutons

Tear lettuce into bite-sized pieces in a large salad bowl. Mix all remaining ingredients, except the croutons, in a small bowl; whisk together until well blended. Refrigerate until ready to use. When ready to serve, pour dressing over lettuce and toss gently. Garnish with croutons.

BACON AND GREEN BEAN SALAD

2 cups fresh green beans, cut
1/2 cup olive oil
1/4 cup vinegar
2 T. onion, minced
1 tsp. seasoned salt
1 head of lettuce, shredded.

Cook beans until tender; drain and cool. Combine oil, vinegar, onion and salt. Pour over beans and chill. Cook bacon until crisp; drain and crumble. Combine beans, lettuce and bacon. Gently toss together and serve.

WHALEHEAD WILTED LETTUCE SALAD

6 slices of bacon
1 head of leaf lettuce, cleaned and dried
1 medium onion, thinly sliced
1/4 cup vinegar
1-1/2 tsp. sugar
1/2 tsp. dry mustard
1/4 tsp. salt
Dash of pepper
2 eggs hard cooked, chopped

Tear lettuce into bite-sized pieces. Fry bacon in a large frying pan; drain, cool; set aside. Discard all but 1/4 cup bacon drippings. Crumble bacon; return to frying pan with onion slices. Add all remaining ingredients, except hard cooked eggs to the frying pan. Bring mixture to a boil stirring constantly. Remove from heat; add lettuce and toss until lettuce is slightly wilted and coated with dressing. Garnish with hard cooked eggs.

TOMATOES AND FRESH MOZZARELLA

5 large ripe tomatoes
2 pkgs. fresh mozzarella
1/4 cup Extra Virgin Olive Oil
1 T. dried oregano
Salt and pepper to taste

Mix oregano and olive oil together. Slice the fresh mozzarella into 1/4" thick slices; lay flat in a shallow glass dish, drizzle the oil mixture over the cheese. Cut 1/2" thick slices of tomato; place on top of the cheese. Sprinkle with salt and pepper; drizzle remaining oil mixture over tomatoes. Cover with plastic wrap and chill or serve immediately.

CROATAN CRAB SALAD

1 pound fresh lump crab meat
1 head lettuce
1/4 tsp. salt
4 tomatoes, quartered
3 eggs, hard cooked and sliced
1 cucumber, sliced
1 cup mayonnaise
3 T. catsup
2 T. relish
2 T. fresh lemon juice

Shred lettuce into a large salad bowl and sprinkle with salt. Arrange crab meat, tomatoes, eggs and cucumber on lettuce. In a separate bowl, combine mayonnaise, catsup, relish and lemon juice. Spread dressing mixture over lettuce. Cover and chill thoroughly. Toss together just before serving.

SHRIMP SALAD

2 pounds cooked shrimp
1 cup dressing
2 cups cooked rice
3/4 cup mayonnaise
2 T. onion, diced
2 T. curry powder
1 T. Dijon mustard
Salt and pepper to taste

Cook, peel and de-vein shrimp; set aside. Place shrimp in a shallow glass dish and marinate in 1/2 cup dressing. Cover and refrigerate for 30 minutes. In a large bowl, toss rice with remainder of ingredients. Add shrimp; chill.

Dressing

6 T. olive oil
1 T. Dijon mustard
1 clove of garlic, minced
2 T. fresh lemon juice

Combine all ingredients in blender; mix well.

JOLLY ROGER'S RICE AND SHRIMP SALAD

1/4 cup onion, grated
2 T. olive oil
1 T. vinegar
1/2 tsp. curry powder
1 T. parsley, chopped
1 tsp. salt
1/4 tsp. pepper
1-1/2 cups cooked rice
1 cup celery, diced
1 pound cooked shrimp
1/4 cup green pepper, chopped
1/2 cup mayonnaise

Peel, de-vein and chop shrimp; chill. Combine onion, oil, vinegar, curry powder, parsley, salt and pepper in a large bowl; mix well. Add rice, toss gently. Chill for 2 hours. Add shrimp and remaining ingredients when ready to serve and toss gently.

Henry Avery

Black Bart

Thomas Tew

Blackbeard

A symbol of fear and almost always certain death, the Jolly Roger was the familiar skull and crossbones flag flown by pirates. The symbol of the skull usually meant that death was imminent. If a spear or dart was included in the flag, this was a sure indication that a violent death would ensue. An hourglass meant time was running out and a raised fist showed a willingness to kill. If the flag was all-inclusive; containing not only a skull and spear, but also a bleeding heart, than a slow, painful death would certainly occur.

WHALEBONE ONION AND TOMATO SLICES

6 tomatoes, thinly sliced
3 medium sweet onions, thinly sliced
1/4 cup green onion, chopped
1/4 cup parsley, chopped
2/3 cup oil
1/4 cup wine vinegar
1 tsp. salt
1/2 tsp. oregano
1/2 tsp. thyme
1/2 tsp. black pepper
1/4 tsp. garlic powder

Combine all ingredients except tomatoes and onion in shallow dish. Add tomato and onion and cover. Marinate overnight in refrigerator. Serve cold.

JAKE McCRACKEN'S CUCUMBER AND TOMATOES

2 firm, medium sized cucumbers, preferably long and thin
4-5 medium sized tomatoes
1/2 cup sour cream
Salt and pepper to taste

Peel cucumbers; cut in half lengthwise, then cut in half lengthwise again. Cut cucumbers into 1" pieces and place in a large bowl. Add sour cream and mix to cover all the pieces. Cut tomatoes into 1" pieces; add to cucumbers and mix gently. Set aside for 10 minutes and stir again. Sprinkle with salt and pepper just before serving. Serves 4.

SEAFOOD ENTRÉES

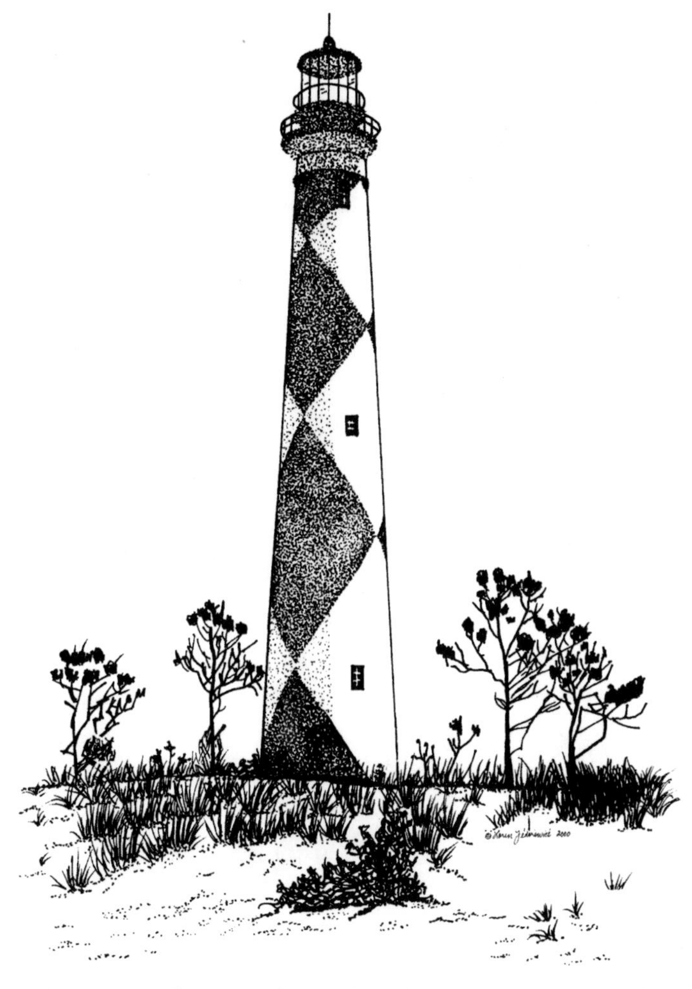

Situated on the Core Banks in North Carolina, the Cape Lookout Lighthouse is part of the Cape Lookout National Seashore. Built in 1859, the Cape Lookout Lighthouse with its distinctive black and white painted checkers is 169 feet tall. Still in service today, the Cape Lookout Lighthouse with its third-order Fresnel lens is visible for nineteen miles.

CRAB HATTERAS

2 cups cooked crabmeat, flaked
3 T. butter
3 T. flour
1 cup chicken broth
1/2 cup cream
1 cup Cheddar cheese, shredded
4 oz. can of sliced mushrooms, drained
3 T. sherry
Salt and pepper to taste
Paprika to taste

Melt butter in a large saucepan; stir in flour, chicken broth and cream stirring constantly over medium heat until thickened. Add cheese and stir until melted. Add mushrooms, sherry, crabmeat and seasonings. Heat thoroughly over low heat. Serve over pasta, rice or toast. Serves 4.

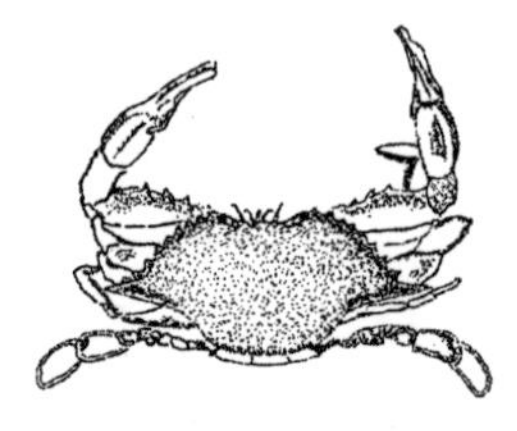

The Blue Crab, a Crustacean, is a bottom dwelling animal that scavenges for food at the bottom of the ocean. The Blue Crab's nickname is Callinectes, which means "beautiful swimmer" in Greek. Although these animals have a striking olive-green back and white belly, they actually received their name from the large, distinctive, bright blue claws that they possess. Blue Crabs have ten legs and are related to the shrimp and lobster. They are an important economic factor because of the delicious meat that they supply.

PORTSMOUTH ISLAND CRAB BURGERS

1 cup cooked crab, flaked
2 T. fresh lemon juice
2 T. onion, chopped
2 T. red or green pepper, chopped
1 cup Cheddar cheese, shredded
1/2 cup catsup
1/2 tsp. salt
1/4 tsp. Worcestershire
4 hamburger buns

Sprinkle crab with lemon juice; mix with remaining ingredients. Spread the bottom half of hamburger bun with the mixture and top with cheese. Broil 4" from heating element until cheese is melted. Cover with hamburger bun top and serve with pickles and chips.

COROLLA DEVILED CRABS

1 pound cooked crabmeat
1 T. green pepper, finely chopped
1 T. onion, chopped
4 T. butter
2 T. flour
1 cup milk
1 T. parsley, minced
1/2 tsp. dried mustard
1 tsp. salt
Dash of white, black, and cayenne
1 tsp. fresh lemon juice
2 hard cooked eggs
Bread crumbs
Clean clam shells for stuffing

Sauté green pepper and onion in 2 tablespoons of butter until lightly browned. Combine flour, and milk; cook until thickened, stirring occasionally. Add sautéed onions, celery, parsley, dry mustard, salt, a dash of white, black and cayenne pepper; add lemon juice. Crumble hard cooked eggs and 1 or 2 tablespoons bread crumbs over crabmeat. Mix sauce with crabmeat and fill prepared shells. Place a pat of butter on top of the mixture; sprinkle with bread crumbs. Place in broiler approximately 4" from the element and broil until lightly browned.

CURRITUCK CRAB CAKES

1 pound cooked crab meat, flaked
1 T. parsley, chopped
3 T. mayonnaise
1/2 tsp. prepared mustard
1/4 tsp. cayenne
1/2 tsp. salt
1 T. Worcestershire
1 cup fresh bread crumbs
1 egg, lightly beaten
1/2 cup butter

In a large bowl combine parsley, mayonnaise, mustard, cayenne, salt and Worcestershire; mix well. Stir in bread crumbs and egg. Add crab meat and mix until well combined. Form into 6 patties. Cover with plastic wrap and refrigerate for 1 hour. Sauté crab cakes in butter until golden on both sides. Serves 6.

CAROLINA DEVILED CRAB

4 slices buttered toast
1/2 cup hot water
1 pound crab meat, flaked
1 medium onion, grated
2 eggs, lightly beaten
1 T. Worcestershire
1 T. catsup
Salt and pepper to taste
2 T. butter

Preheat oven to 350° F. Grease 4 crab shells or individual casseroles. Cut toast into small pieces and place in mixing bowl; add hot water to soften. Stir in crab meat, onion, eggs, Worcestershire and catsup; season with salt and pepper; mix well. Spoon into shells or individual casseroles. Dot with butter. Bake uncovered for 30 minutes. Serves 6.

FRISCO FRIED CRABS

Oil for deep frying
12 soft-shell crabs
1 cup sifted flour
1 T. Creole seasoning
1/2 tsp. salt
1/4 tsp. pepper
Milk
2 eggs, lightly beaten
1 cup bread crumbs
Lemon wedges

Carefully clean crabs under cold running water and pat dry with a paper towel. Sprinkle with salt and pepper; cover with milk and soak for about 30 minutes; drain crabs. Mix salt, pepper and Creole seasoning in flour. Completely coat crabs with flour mixture; dip in beaten eggs and roll in bread crumbs. In a large saucepan or deep fryer, preheat oil to 360° F and carefully place crabs in the pan, in batches; cook for 2–3 minutes. Turn crabs over and fry for another 2–3 minutes or until golden brown. Drain on paper toweling. Garnish with lemon wedges. Serves 6.

CRAB NEWBURG

1 pound fresh lump crab meat
1/2 cup butter
3 T. flour
1/2 tsp. salt
1/2 tsp. paprika
Dash of cayenne
2 T. onion, finely chopped
2 cups cream
3 egg yolks, lightly beaten
2 T. sherry
6 slices buttered toast

In a large bowl, break up crab meat being cautious not to make the piece too small. Check for pieces of shell or cartilage. Melt butter in saucepan over medium heat. Stir in flour, seasonings and onion. Gradually add cream. Cook, stirring constantly, until thickened and smooth. Reduce heat; add crab meat. Heat thoroughly; do not boil. Serve over toast. Serves 6.

SAUTEÉD CRAB CUTLETS

1 cup WHITE SAUCE,
(see page 20)
1/2 tsp. salt
1/4 tsp. pepper
1 egg
Dash of celery salt
1 T. onion, grated
2 cups cooked crab meat, flaked
Flour
1/3 cup mayonnaise
3/4 cup bread crumbs
1/2 cup butter
CHEESE SAUCE, *see page 20*
Lemon wedges

In medium saucepan, blend White Sauce, salt, pepper, egg, celery salt and onion. Bring to boil over low heat, stirring constantly. Simmer for 2 minutes. Remove from heat. Stir in crab meat. Spread on large plate. Refrigerate until cool. Divide cooled mixture into 6 parts. Shape each like a cutlet or round cake. Coat both sides with flour; cover both sides completely with mayonnaise. Dip in crumbs; press crumbs with a spatula or a knife blade. Reshape, if necessary. Melt butter in large frying pan; sauté crab cakes about 10 minutes, or until golden on both sides. Arrange on serving dish. Serve with Cheese Sauce and lemon wedges. Serves 6.

STUFFED CRABS

18 hard-shell crabs
1/2 cup butter
1 clove garlic, crushed.
2 T. onion, finely chopped
2 T. celery, finely chopped
2 T. scallions, minced
1-1/2 cups fresh bread crumbs
2 T. parsley, chopped
1 tsp. Creole seasoning
1 cup dry bread crumbs
1/2 tsp. salt
Butter

Scald crabs. Remove meat and set aside. Boil shells in water then thoroughly clean with stiff brush. Preheat oven to 400° F. Arrange empty shells on baking sheet. In a medium frying pan, melt butter; sauté garlic, onion, celery and scallions over medium heat for 5 minutes. Remove from heat. Crumble crab meat; mix with fresh bread crumbs, parsley, Creole seasoning and salt. Arrange mixture in crab shells. Dot the mixture with a pat of butter and sprinkle with dry bread crumbs. Bake for 20 minutes or until tops are golden. Serves 6.

TEACH'S DEVILED CRAB

1/4 cup butter
2 T. flour
1 tsp. dry mustard
1 tsp. salt
1/4 tsp. pepper
1 T. parsley, chopped
1 cup milk
1 pound cooked crab meat
2 eggs, hard cooked and chopped
2 tsp. fresh lemon juice
1/2 cup cracker crumbs
2 T. melted butter

Preheat oven to 425° F. Grease 6 crab shells. Melt 1/4 cup butter in medium saucepan. Stir in flour, mustard, salt, pepper and parsley. Gradually stir in milk. Cook over low heat, stirring constantly until thickened and smooth. Stir in crab meat and eggs. Heat to serving temperature. Remove from heat. Stir in lemon juice; spoon into shells. Sprinkle with cracker crumbs and melted butter. Bake for 15 minutes, or until browned. Serves 6.

MACKAY ISLAND EGG AND CRAB SALAD

1 cup crab meat, flaked
1 cup fresh bread crumbs
1 cup light cream
1-1/2 cups mayonnaise
6 eggs, hard cooked and diced
1 T. onion, grated
1/2 tsp. salt
1/4 tsp. pepper
1/2 cup buttered bread crumbs

Preheat oven to 350° F. Grease 8 crab shells or individual casseroles. In mixing bowl combine all ingredients except buttered crumbs; mix well. Spoon into shells or casseroles. Sprinkle with buttered crumbs. Bake in preheated oven for 20 minutes, or until golden. Serves 8.

Found along the Atlantic Coast, the Brown Pelican, known as a tame and trusting bird, is one of two species of pelican that plunge-dive for fish. Their most distinguishable characteristic is the large bill-pouch formed by very elastic skin. This skin has the ability to become greatly distended and is therefore capable of holding large quantities of water or food.

KEVIN'S CRAB PIE

1-1/2 cups seasoned stuffing mix
3/4 cup melted butter
3 T. scallions, finely chopped
1/4 cup flour
1-1/2 cups milk
1-1/2 cups cooked crab meat, flaked
2 T. roasted red peppers, chopped
1/4 tsp. dry mustard
Salt and pepper to taste
1/2 cup sour cream
Finely chopped parsley, for garnish

Preheat oven to 425° F. Grease 8" inch pie plate. Crush stuffing mix with rolling pin or process in food processor; put in pie plate. Stir 1/4 cup of the butter into crumbs. Press mixture on bottom and sides of pie plate. Melt remaining butter in saucepan; sauté scallions. Sprinkle scallions with flour; gradually stir in milk; cook over medium heat, stirring constantly, until thickened and smooth. Stir in crab meat, roasted peppers and mustard; season with salt and pepper. Remove from heat. Stir in sour cream. Gently spoon mixture into prepared pie plate. Bake for 10 minutes. Sprinkle with parsley just before serving. Serves 4 to 6.

BAKED BLUEFISH

1 bluefish, 4–5 pounds, cleaned and split
Extra virgin olive oil
Juice of 1 fresh lemon
2 T. parsley, chopped

Preheat oven to 375° F. Oil a baking dish with olive oil and place the fish skin side down. Pour the lemon juice over the fish. Drizzle a little more olive oil over the top of the fish before baking to help keep it moist. Bake for 25 minutes or until fish is opaque and flakes easily with a fork. Serve with lemon wedges and a sprinkling of parsley. Serves 4.

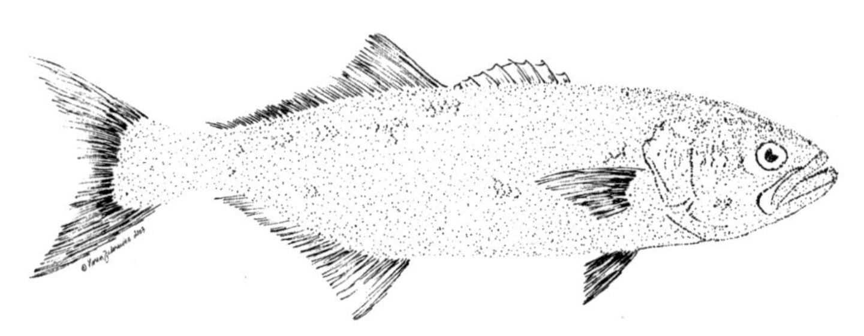

The long, slender Bluefish has very sharp teeth and its body is a bright, greenish-blue hue with a striking silver-white belly. Bluefish prefer deeper waters and warmer water currents where they are voracious feeders, often invoking a feeding frenzy within their large schools. More often than not, they are likely to strike more fish than they can consume. Having the reputation of being an incredibly strong fighting fish with vicious striking habits the Bluefish is a popular sport fish and a popular food dish.

FRIED SHRIMP

Oil for frying.

1 pound cooked shrimp

Batter for fried shrimp:
1 egg
1-1/4 cups of flour
1 tsp. baking powder
1 cup water
1 tsp. salt

Peel shrimp. Split lengthwise and leave the tail on. In a mixing bowl, beat egg, add water; stir in dry ingredients; mix well. Heat oil to 365°F. Dip shrimp into batter and fry until golden brown. Serves 3 to 4.

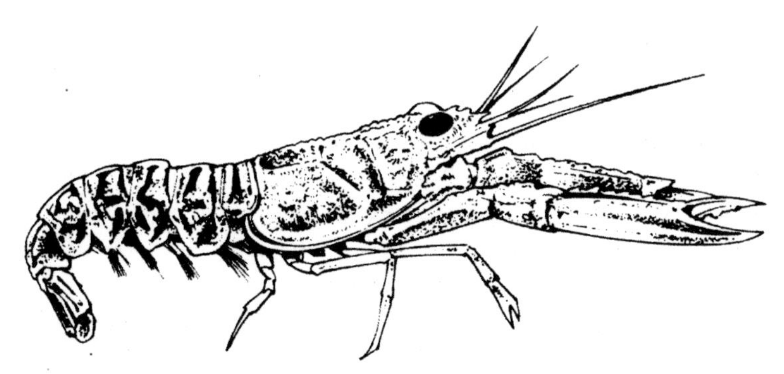

Known as a Crustacean, Shrimp are shallow water and ocean scavengers, encountering food on the bottom of the ocean. Shrimp have chewing mouthparts and are bluish-gray in appearance. They have a slightly transparent outer shell, or "exoskeleton", which is a rigid outer shell that provides protection for the soft internal tissue. Since their exoskeleton does not grow, a shrimp will molt and then replace it. They have 10 feet and a long, strong tail which allows mobility in the form of walking or swimming (backwards). Shrimp are important to the world economically because they are frequently harvested for their hearty, delicious meat.

SHOALS BROILED SHRIMP

2 pounds fresh shrimp
1/2 cup butter, melted
2 cloves garlic, minced
2 tsp. salt
1/2 cup parsley, chopped
Lemon wedges

Peel and de-vein shrimp. Place shrimp in a shallow baking pan; sprinkle with melted butter, garlic, salt and half of the parsley. Broil about 4" from heating element for 5 to 7 minutes on each side, depending on size of shrimp. Sprinkle with remaining parsley. Serve with lemon wedges. Serves 4.

ATLANTIC STEAMED SHRIMP

1-1/2 pounds fresh shrimp
1 cup water
1 tsp. seafood seasoning
1 tsp. salt

In a large saucepan, bring water, salt and seafood seasoning to a boil. Add shrimp; allow water to return to a boil. Cook the shrimp for 2 minutes. Remove from heat, cover and let shrimp stand for 5 minutes. Serve warm or place shrimp in an ice water bath to chill and serve cold. Serves 4.

CHICAMACOMICO CREOLE SHRIMP

2 cups cooked shrimp
4 T. butter
1/2 cup celery, diced
1/2 cup onion, chopped
1/3 cup green pepper, chopped
2 cups tomatoes, diced
1 tsp. salt
1/4 tsp. pepper
3 T. Worcestershire sauce
1 garlic clove, crushed
1/3 tsp. paprika
1 T. fresh lemon juice
2 T. parsley, minced
3 T. flour
1 tsp. celery seed
2 bay leaves

Peel and de-vein shrimp; set aside. Melt butter in saucepan; sauté celery, onion and green pepper until tender, add parsley and flour. When flour is well blended, add tomatoes and remaining seasonings. Add shrimp. Cover and cook over low heat for 10 minutes. Serve over rice. Serves 4.

The first of seven Lifesaving Stations constructed along North Carolina's Outer Banks, Chicamacomico was built in 1874. Chicamacomico was a simple wooden building used for boat storage and living quarters for the men of the U.S. Lifesaving Service. The crews at Chicamacomico performed many outstanding rescues during its operation including the burning British tanker, Mirlo during World War I. The U.S. Lifesaving Service was replaced by the United States Coast Guard in 1915.

SOUTHERN SHORES SHRIMP SAUTÉ

2 pounds fresh shrimp
1 stick butter
2 cloves garlic, minced
Juice of 1 lemon
1/3 cup parsley, minced
1 T. chives, chopped
Salt and pepper to taste
Dash of Worcestershire

Peel and de-vein shrimp; set aside. In large saucepan, melt butter and sauté garlic. Add shrimp, lemon juice, salt, pepper and Worcestershire sauce. Cook over medium heat, stirring occasionally until shrimp turns pink. Reduce cooking liquid from shrimp, but do not overcook. Serve over rice. Garnish with parsley and chives before serving. Serves 4 to 6.

SKEWERED SHRIMP

1 pound fresh shrimp
1 - 15oz. can of pineapple chunks
1 large red or green pepper, cut into 1-inch squares
1 cup onion, chopped
8 oz. can tomato sauce
1/2 cup water
1/4 cup brown sugar
1/4 cup oil
1/4 cup fresh lemon juice
3 T. Worcestershire sauce
2 T. mustard
2 tsp. salt
1/4 tsp. pepper

Peel and de-vein shrimp; set aside. Sauté onions in a saucepan until tender. Add tomato sauce, water, brown sugar, oil, lemon juice, Worcestershire sauce, mustard, salt, and pepper. Simmer, uncovered, 15 minutes, stirring once or twice. Set aside to cool. Drain pineapple, reserving 2 tablespoons of the syrup. Combine syrup with sauce mixture. Place shrimp in a resealable plastic bag. Pour sauce mixture over shrimp, seal bag and marinate in the refrigerator for 2 to 3 hours. Drain; reserve sauce. Preheat both sides of grill on high for 10 minutes. Thread the shrimp, pineapple chunks, and pepper squares on skewers. Place on grill. Cook for 10 to 15 minute, basting frequently with marinade until shrimp are done. Serves 4.

BLACKBEARD'S BOURBON SHRIMP

1-1/2 pounds of fresh shrimp
1 T. butter
1 small onion, chopped
2 T. bourbon
1 green and red pepper, chopped
Dash of celery salt
1 can of stewed tomatoes, juice included
1 fresh tomato, chopped
8 oz. container sour cream
Parsley flakes

Peel and de-vein shrimp. Cook shrimp, drain and set aside. In a medium saucepan, melt butter and sauté onions until tender. Add bourbon; simmer for 10 minutes. Add chopped peppers, celery salt, and parsley flakes. Mix in stewed tomatoes and chopped fresh tomato. Cook over medium heat until hot. Add shrimp and slowly mix in sour cream until well blended. Reduce heat and continue cooking until heated through. Serve over rice. Serves 3 to 4.

One of the fiercest pirates in history, Edward Teach, also known as Blackbeard, prowled the Atlantic Coast on his ship, the Queen Anne's Revenge. Pillaging towns and frightening people, Blackbeard supposedly buried his treasure in many places including his headquarters at Teach's Hole on Ocracoke Island in North Carolina. Legend has it when Blackbeard was decapitated in 1718 by Lieutenant Robert Maynard of the British Royal Navy, his body when thrown overboard, swam around the sloop three times before sinking.

CAPE LOOKOUT SHRIMP SCAMPI

1 cup olive oil
1/2 cup dry white wine
1/2 tsp. oregano
2 cloves garlic, crushed
2 pounds large shrimp

Peel and de-vein shrimp; set aside. In mixing bowl, blend oil, wine, oregano and garlic; add shrimp. Cover with plastic wrap; refrigerate for 4 to 6 hours; stir occasionally. Preheat broiler. Line broiling pan with aluminum foil. Place shrimp and marinade on broiling pan. Broil 4 to 5 inches from heat for 7 minutes. Turn shrimp; broil for 10 minutes longer. Serve shrimp with marinade. Serves 6.

OCRACOKE INLET SHRIMP

2 pounds fresh large shrimp
Salt and pepper to taste
Flour
2 large eggs, beaten
3/4 cup butter
2 cups fresh mushrooms, sliced
1/4 cup dry white wine

Peel and de-vein shrimp; rinse in cold water; drain and pat dry. Season with salt and pepper; Dip in eggs, coat with flour. Melt 1/2 cup of the butter in large frying pan; sauté shrimp over medium heat, turning frequently, until golden. Meanwhile, melt remaining butter in another frying pan; sauté mushrooms for 5 minutes. When shrimp are golden, stir in mushrooms; add wine. Cook over medium heat, stirring frequently, for another 2 minutes. Serves 4.

SHRIMP DE JONGHE

4 pounds fresh shrimp
1 cup butter
2 cloves garlic, minced
2/3 cup parsley, chopped
1/2 tsp. paprika
Dash of Tabasco
1/2 cup sweet sherry
2 cups fresh bread crumbs

Peel and de-vein shrimp; set aside. Preheat oven to 325° F. Grease 9"x13" baking pan. Place shrimp in baking pan. Melt butter in saucepan; remove from heat. Stir in garlic, half the parsley, paprika, Tabasco and sherry. Add crumbs; toss lightly. Spoon crumb mixture over shrimp. Bake uncovered for 20 to 25 minutes, or until browned. Sprinkle with remaining parsley before serving. Serves 8.

ANNE BONNY'S FRIED SHRIMP

Oil for deep frying

2 pounds shrimp
Salt
2 eggs
2 T. water
1 cup bread crumbs
Lemon wedges

Peel and de-vein shrimp, leaving last joint of shell and tail on. Drain shrimp on paper toweling. Sprinkle with salt. In small bowl, beat eggs and water. Dip shrimp in eggs; coat completely. Dip in crumbs, coating well. Fry shrimp in oil heated to 365° F for about 5 minutes, or until golden. Drain on paper toweling. Serve with lemon wedges or favorite cocktail sauce. Serves 6.

SPRINGERS POINT SHRIMP

1/3 cup olive oil
1-1/2 cup onions, chopped
1-1/2 cup green pepper, chopped
1/2 cup celery, chopped
1 clove garlic, crushed
2 T. flour
1 tsp. salt
1/4 tsp. pepper
Dash of cayenne
1 bay leaf, crushed
1 large can tomatoes
1-1/2 pounds fresh shrimp
1 tsp. sugar
1/4 cup parsley, chopped
Cooked rice

Peel and de-vein shrimp; set aside. Heat oil in large frying pan; sauté onions, green pepper, celery and garlic for 5 minutes. Stir in flour, salt, pepper, cayenne, bay leaf and tomatoes. Bring to boil; cover; lower heat and simmer for 20 minutes. Add shrimp, sugar and parsley. Cover; simmer for 5 to 7 minutes, or until shrimp turn pink. Serve over rice. Serves 4.

PAMLICO POACHED SHRIMP

2 pounds shrimp
2 cups water
1 cup vinegar
2 bay leaves
1 T. salt
2 T. dry mustard
2 T. mustard seed
2 T. celery seed
1 tsp. pepper

Prepare bouillon: In saucepan combine water, vinegar, bay leaves, salt, mustard, mustard seed, celery seed and pepper. Bring to boil. Simmer for 10 minutes. Peel and de-vein shrimp and add to bouillon. Cover; simmer for 5 to 7 minutes, stirring occasionally. Drain. Serve hot or cold. Serves 6 to 8.

SHRIMP ITALIANO

3-1/2 pounds fresh shrimp
7 slices bacon
1/4 tsp. garlic powder
1 cup onions, chopped
1 pound fresh mushrooms, sliced
2-28 oz. cans Italian tomatoes
6 oz. can tomato paste
1 can beef consommé
1 tsp. oregano
1 tsp. basil
1 tsp. salt
1/4 tsp. pepper
1 T. sugar
1 T. prepared mustard
1/4 cup flour
1/2 cup water
Cooked rice
Chopped parsley

Cook bacon in large frying pan until crisp. Drain on paper towel, crumble and set aside. Sprinkle remaining bacon drippings with garlic powder. Add shrimp that has been peeled and de-veined; sauté for 3 minutes. Add onions and mushrooms; sauté for a few minutes longer. Add tomatoes, tomato paste, consommé, seasonings, sugar, mustard and bacon. Simmer for 10 minutes, stirring frequently. Combine flour and water; stir into sauce and cook until flour cooks down and sauce is thickened. Serve over rice and sprinkle with parsley. Serves 8.

SALVO STUFFED FRIED SHRIMP

Oil for frying

2 T. oil
1 large onion, finely chopped
1/2 cup celery, finely chopped
1 clove garlic, crushed
1/4 cup green pepper, finely chopped
2 cups crab meat, flaked
2 T. scallions, finely chopped
2 T. parsley, finely chopped
4 eggs
1/4 cup flour
1/2 tsp. salt
1/8 tsp. cayenne
1/8 tsp. pepper
24 large shrimp
1 cup cracker crumbs

Prepare Crab Meat Stuffing: Heat oil in large frying pan; sauté onion, celery, garlic and green pepper over low heat for 5 minutes. Stir in crab meat, scallions, parsley, 2 eggs, flour, salt, cayenne and pepper. Cook over low heat, stirring constantly, until thickened and comes together. Remove from heat. Cool. Peel and de-vein shrimp. Cut deeply down the back but not through shrimp. Press about 1 tablespoon stuffing into each shrimp. Roll in crumbs. Beat remaining eggs; dip shrimp first in eggs, then in crumbs. Fry shrimp in oil heated to 365° F for 4 minutes, or until golden brown. Drain on paper towel. Serve with lemon wedges and favorite cocktail sauce. Serves 6.

SHRIMP TEMPURA

Oil for frying

1 pound fresh shrimp
1-1/2 cups flour
1 tsp. baking powder
Pinch of salt
Pinch of sugar
2 T. solid shortening
2 eggs
1 cup milk

Peel shrimp, leaving tails intact. With sharp knife, slit shrimp deeply down back without cutting all the way through; de-vein. Rinse shrimp under cold running water and place on paper towel. Cover with another towel. In medium mixing bowl, sift together dry ingredients. Cut in shortening until mixture resembles fine crumbs. Stir in eggs and milk; mix until blended and batter is fairly thick. Hold shrimp by the tail and dip in batter. Fry a few shrimp at a time in oil heated to 365° F for about 3 minutes, or until golden brown. Drain on paper toweling. Serve with favorite dipping sauce or cocktail sauce. Serves 4.

RODANTHE SHRIMP ROYALE

2 T. cooking oil
1 large onion, chopped
3 stalks celery, chopped
4 oz. can sliced mushrooms
2 T. soy sauce
1 pound shrimp, peeled and de-veined
1 T. cornstarch, mixed with 2 T. water
Cooked rice

Heat oil in saucepan; sauté onion and celery until onion is transparent. Add mushrooms and soy sauce; simmer for 20 minutes. Add shrimp. Stir in cornstarch. Simmer for 10 minutes longer until sauce is thickened and clear. Serve over rice. Serves 4.

HATTERASMAN SHRIMP

1 cup White Sauce (see page 20)
1 cup grated Cheddar cheese
1 large can tomatoes, drained
1 cup cooked shrimp, diced
Salt and pepper to taste
1/2 tsp. paprika
4 slices toast

Place White Sauce in saucepan; add cheese, tomatoes and shrimp. Season with salt and pepper; add paprika. Cook over medium heat, stirring constantly, until cheese is melted and sauce bubbles. Serve over toast. Serves 4.

SHRIMP THERMIDOR

1 pound cooked shrimp, peeled, de-veined
1/2 cup butter
1/2 cup fresh mushrooms, sliced
1/4 cup flour
1 tsp. salt
1/2 tsp. dry mustard
Dash of cayenne
2 cups milk
Grated Parmesan cheese
Paprika

Preheat oven to 400° F. Grease individual baking shells. Cut shrimp in half lengthwise. Melt butter in saucepan; sauté mushrooms for 5 minutes. Stir in flour, salt, mustard and cayenne. Gradually stir in milk. Cook, stirring constantly, until thickened and smooth. Stir in shrimp. Divide into shells or ramekins. Sprinkle with cheese and paprika. Bake for 10 minutes, or until cheese is browned. Serves 6.

SHRIMP NEWBURG

4 T. butter
2-1/2 T. flour
2 cups cream
6 T. catsup
1-1/2 T. Worcestershire
2 pounds shrimp, peeled, deveined and cooked
Salt, paprika and cayenne to taste
4 T. sherry
Cooked rice or unbuttered toast

Melt butter in saucepan over medium heat. Stir in flour; cook 2–3 minutes stirring frequently until flour is cooked down. Slowly stir in cream. Cook, stirring constantly, until thickened and smooth. Stir in catsup and Worcestershire. Add shrimp. Heat thoroughly. Season with salt, paprika and cayenne. Stir in sherry just before serving. Serve over rice or toast. Serves 6.

CAPTAIN DAVE'S SHRIMP DELIGHT

1-1/2 pounds fresh shrimp
2 T. fresh lemon juice
1/2 cup melted butter
1/2 cup bread crumbs
1 garlic clove, minced
2 T. fresh parsley, minced
1 T. Parmesan cheese
1 T. oregano

Preheat oven to 350° F. Peel and de-vein shrimp and place in a buttered 9" pie plate; sprinkle with lemon juice. In a separate bowl, combine melted butter with breadcrumbs, garlic, parsley and oregano. Spoon mixture over shrimp; bake uncovered for 15 minutes. Sprinkle with parmesan cheese and broil for 3 minutes until bread crumbs are lightly browned. Serves 3 to 4.

GRILLED MAHI MAHI

4 Mahi Mahi fillets
1 clove garlic, minced
1/4 cup olive oil
Salt and pepper to taste

Rub the fillets with olive oil. Season with salt, pepper, and garlic. Clean grill and preheat on high so it is hot. Place the Mahi Mahi on the preheated grill. Once on the grill, leave it untouched for 4 to 5 minutes. Grill 4 to 5 minutes per side. Fish flakes easily when done. Serves 4.

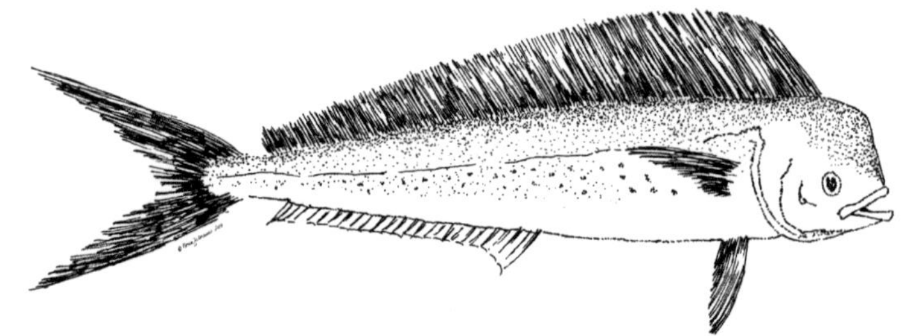

A brilliantly colored fish, the Dolphin or Mahi Mahi is a very strong swimmer and a fast moving game fish. The Dolphin fish is distinguishable because of a high, blunt forehead and a blue-green body complimented by bright, golden-yellow sides. The Dolphin fish seeks temperate waters and can often be seen traveling in small schools, or hiding among patches of floating seaweed. The Dolphin fish is considered both a popular game fish and a rich food source, because of its speed and high jumps, and delicious meat, respectively.

GRILLED TUNA STEAKS

4 tuna steaks, 8 oz. each

Salt and pepper to taste
1/4 cup olive oil

Rub steaks with olive oil, salt and pepper. Place tuna steaks on clean preheated grill (or tuna might stick). Grill tuna steaks 3 to 5 minutes on each side. Serves 4.

The beautiful Yellow fin tuna is highly distinguishable because of its long, vibrant yellow dorsal fin. Its torpedo shaped body embraces a bluish-black on top with yellow and silver on its sides and belly. Found worldwide in warmer waters, Yellow fin tuna are often found in schools along with other tuna species. The Yellow fin tuna is considered both an excellent food dish and sport fish because of its strength and endurance.

HOT TUNA BUNS

1 cup fresh tuna, cooked and flaked
1/2 cup mayonnaise
1/4 cup onion, chopped
2 T. relish
4 hamburger buns
1 cup cheddar cheese, shredded

Combine first 4 ingredients together in a small bowl. Spread 1/4 cup of the tuna mixture on the bottom half of the hamburger bun and top with cheese. Broil 4" from heating unit for 3 minutes or until cheese is melted. Cover with the top of the bun and serve. Serves 4.

TUNA PITA SANDWICH

1 cup fresh tuna, cooked and flaked
1/2 cup mayonnaise
1/2 cup green pepper, chopped
1/2 cup red onion, chopped
1 cup celery, chopped
1/4 cup water chestnuts, minced
1 pkg. pita bread
Alfalfa sprouts (optional)

Mix all ingredients in medium bowl except pita bread. Cut pita bread in half and open to form pockets. Fill pockets with tuna mixture and top with sprouts.

SILVER LAKE TUNA SANDWICHES

1/2 pound fresh tuna, cooked and flaked
1-1/2 cups mayonnaise
Dash of Tabasco
1 tsp. Worcestershire
1 tsp. fresh lemon juice
1/4 tsp. pepper
4 slices bread, toasted
1/4 cup butter
Tomatoes, sliced thick
2 eggs, hard cooked and halved lengthwise

In bowl blend tuna, 1/2 cup of mayonnaise, Tabasco, Worcestershire, lemon juice and pepper. Set aside. Preheat broiler. Line broiling pan with aluminum foil. Arrange toast on broiling pan. Top each piece with sliced tomato, then half an egg. Mound tuna mixture over on egg halves; cover completely with remaining mayonnaise. Place under broiler 4 to 5 inches from heating element. Broil for 7 to 8 minutes, until puffed and golden. Serves 4.

TUNA TERRAPIN

3 T. butter
3 eggs, hard cooked
3 T. flour
3/4 tsp. mustard
1 tsp. salt
2 cups milk
1 cup tuna, flaked
1 pimiento, diced
1 T. green pepper, chopped
4 large olives, diced
1 T. fresh lemon juice
Puff pastry shells, baked

Melt butter in large frying pan over medium heat. Separate egg yolks from whites. Set whites aside. Mash yolks. Add yolks, flour, mustard and salt to butter; mix well. Gradually stir in milk. Cook, stirring constantly, until sauce thickens. Dice egg whites; add to mixture along with remaining ingredients. Cook over low heat until heated through. Serve in pastry shells. Serves 6.

ORVILLE AND WILBUR TUNA FRITTERS

Oil for deep frying

2 cups biscuit mix
1 tsp. seasoned salt
1 egg, lightly beaten
2/3 cup evaporated milk
1 T. fresh lemon juice
1-1/2 cups flaked tuna
2 T. onion, finely chopped
2 T. green pepper, finely chopped
1/2 cup celery, finely chopped
2 T. parsley, chopped
CHEESE SAUCE—*see page 20*

Combine biscuit mix, salt, egg, milk and lemon juice. Add tuna and vegetables; mix well. Drop by teaspoons into oil heated to 365° F. Fry for 1-1/2 to 2 minutes. Turn; fry until golden brown. Drain on paper toweling. Serve with Cheese Sauce.

The Wright Brothers National Memorial in Kitty Hawk, North Carolina, commemorates the first successful flight achieved by the Wright Brothers in the Wright Flyer on December 17, 1903. Built out of gray granite quarried from Mount Airy, North Carolina, the triangular pylon is 60 feet tall. Dedicated as a memorial on November 19, 1932 the Wright Brothers National Memorial, atop Kill Devil Hill, is owned by the National Park Service.

TUNA WITH TOMATO SAUCE

2 pounds fresh tuna, sliced 1-1/2" thick
4 T. olive oil
1 T. parsley, chopped
1 garlic clove, minced
1 small onion, sliced
1/2 can tomato paste
2 cups hot water
Salt and pepper to taste

Sprinkle tuna with salt and pepper. Heat oil in a large frying pan. Sauté onion, garlic and parsley until tender. Blend tomato paste with 2 cups of hot water; add mixture to vegetables. Cover and simmer for 20 minutes, stirring frequently. Add tuna, cover and cook 15 minutes or until tender. Serves 4.

WAHOO

2 Wahoo fillets (1/2" thick)
Juice of 1/2 lemon
Favorite seafood seasoning
1 T. olive oil
Salt and pepper to taste
Minced garlic (optional)

Rub the fillets with lemon juice and season with salt, pepper, garlic and seafood seasoning. Preheat clean grill so it is hot. Brush olive oil on clean grill to prevent the fish from sticking. Grill the fillets for approximately 5 minutes on each side. Cook until opaque. Fish flakes easily when done. Serves 2.

A species of mackerel, the Wahoo is a long, slender, blue-grey fish with large, sharp teeth. Its blue-gray tapered body is marked with a series of brilliant bands running along the sides of its body. Considered one of the fastest fish in the ocean, the Wahoo can easily reach speeds in excess of 40 mph. Although this fish is often found near the surface where the temperate waters reach 72° to 77° F, this beautiful fish also seeks to inhabit its favorite local offshore wreck. The fast swimming Wahoo is not only considered valuable as a sport fish, but also as a food source because of its sweet, white meat.

FRIED OYSTERS

Oil for frying

1 quart oysters, freshly shucked and drained
2 eggs, well beaten
2 T. cream
1 tsp. salt
1/8 pepper
1 cup cornmeal
Tartar Sauce (optional)
Lemon wedges (optional)

Dry oysters on paper toweling. Combine eggs and cream; season with salt and pepper. Dip oysters in egg mixture; gently roll in cornmeal. Fry oysters in a deep frying pan with about 1" of oil heated to 365° F until golden brown on both sides, turning once. Drain on paper toweling. Serve with Tartar Sauce. Garnish with lemon wedges. Serves 6.

The Oyster is a familiar Mollusk that is surrounded by a hard shiny, black and silver shell and is famous for crafting pearls. These animals tend to permanently attach themselves underwater to hard, unmoving surfaces such as large rocks, docks and unused boats. They are also considered "filter feeders," which means they feed on small organisms and debris that float around in the water by siphoning in water over their gills. A piece of sand or debris that remains inside the oyster can instigate the production of a pearl. They are important economically because they are commercially grown for food or cultured for pearls.

BROILED OYSTERS

3/4 cup bread crumbs
1/2 tsp. dry mustard
Dash of cayenne
1/4 tsp. paprika
1/2 tsp. salt
24 oysters, freshly shucked and drained
1/4 cup melted butter
Lemon wedges

Preheat broiler. Grease shallow baking pan. Combine crumbs, mustard, cayenne, paprika and salt. Roll oysters in crumb mixture. Arrange in a single layer in prepared baking pan. Sprinkle with half the butter. Broil until lightly browned. Turn oysters; baste with remaining butter; broil until browned. Serve with lemon wedges. Serves 4.

ROASTED OYSTERS

24 large oysters in shells
Salt and pepper to taste
1/2 cup melted butter

Preheat oven to 450° F. Grease 2 baking sheets. Clean outsides of oysters. Place on baking sheets. Bake for 5 minutes or until shells are easily separated. Remove flat shell. Season oysters with salt, pepper and butter. Serve in shells. Serves 4.

PEA ISLAND OYSTER BOIL

1 bushel oysters in shells
2 cups catsup
1 cup vinegar
1 tsp. salt
1/4 tsp. pepper
2 T. horseradish

Bring water to a boil in a large, deep frying pan. While water is heating prepare dipping sauce. In a mixing bowl blend catsup, vinegar, salt, pepper and horseradish; mix well, set aside. Place oysters in boiling water; leave in water only long enough for oysters to open slightly. Remove oysters and add the next batch. Serve with dipping sauce. Serves 12 to 15.

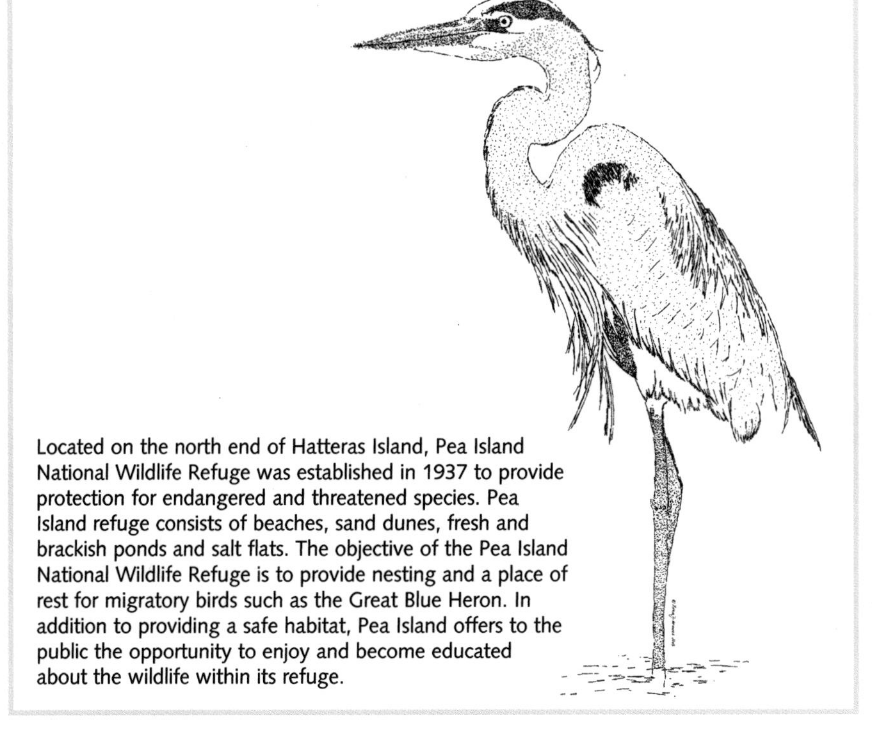

Located on the north end of Hatteras Island, Pea Island National Wildlife Refuge was established in 1937 to provide protection for endangered and threatened species. Pea Island refuge consists of beaches, sand dunes, fresh and brackish ponds and salt flats. The objective of the Pea Island National Wildlife Refuge is to provide nesting and a place of rest for migratory birds such as the Great Blue Heron. In addition to providing a safe habitat, Pea Island offers to the public the opportunity to enjoy and become educated about the wildlife within its refuge.

FORT RALEIGH CREAMED OYSTERS

1/2 cup butter
1/2 cup scallions, chopped
1 pint oysters, freshly shucked and drained
1 T. flour
Salt and pepper to taste
Pinch of Thyme
Toast

Melt all but 1 tablespoon of butter. In a medium saucepan, sauté scallions for 3 minutes, or until tender. Add oysters. Cook over very low heat. Combine reserved butter and flour. Gradually stir in butter-flour mixture as oysters release their juices. Season with salt, pepper and thyme. Oysters are done when the edges begin to curl. Remove from heat and serve immediately over toast.

POMPANO

6 pompano fillets
1/2 tsp. salt
1/2 tsp. pepper
1/4 cup flour
10 T. butter
6 T. oil
2 T. fresh lemon juice
2 T. parsley, chopped
Lemon wedges

Season both sides of fillets with salt and pepper. Dredge in flour. Heat 3 tablespoons butter and oil together a large frying pan; brown fillets. Turn pompano and cook until tender; remove from heat and place on platter. Melt the remaining butter and mix with lemon juice and parsley. Pour over fish and garnish with lemon wedges. Serves 6.

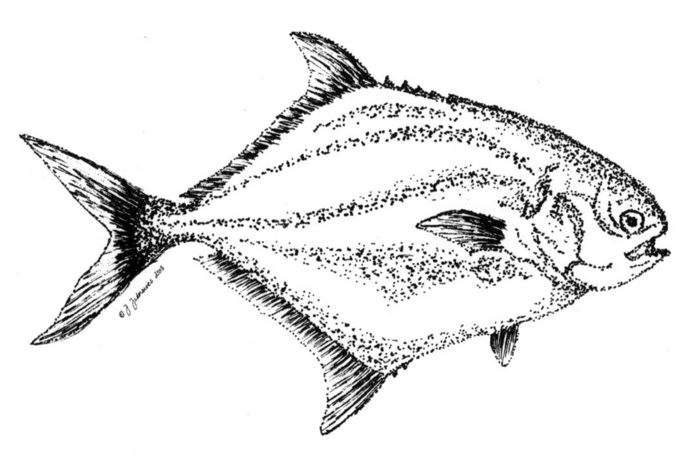

A feisty fish that puts up a good fight, the Pompano is a silver colored fish with a wide body and a short snout. The Pompano is a prized sport fish because of its quickness to strike, long runs in the water and unique characteristic of skipping across the top of the water when they jump. They reside near the shore line because they favor the waves and the sand. The Pompano is considered a gourmet fish because of its delicious flavor and delightful texture.

SAUTEÉD BREADED SCALLOPS

1 pound scallops
Flour for dredging
1 large egg
1 T. water
Bread crumbs or corn meal
2 T. butter
2 T oil
Salt and pepper to taste
Lemon wedges

Dry scallops well on paper toweling. Beat egg with 1 tablespoon water. Roll scallops in flour; dip in egg mixture. Roll scallops in crumbs or corn meal. Heat butter and oil together in a large frying pan; add scallops and sauté until golden brown on both sides. Do not overcook. Sprinkle with salt and pepper. Serve with lemon wedges. Serves 3–4.

Scallops are a type of Mollusk that, unlike other members of its family such as oysters or clams, are not sedentary and can actually propel themselves through the water. These graceful animals live in deeper ocean water and are surrounded by a beautiful whitish-pink shell, which is often associated with the Greek goddess, Venus, who is found standing inside of a giant, open scallop. They are considered "filter feeders," which means they feed on small organisms and debris that float around in the water by siphoning in water over their gills. They are important economically, as they are considered a rich, luscious seafood.

SCALLOPS WITH WHITE WINE SAUCE

1-1/2 pounds scallops
3/4 cup dry white wine
3 T. butter
2 T. flour
1-1/2 cups heavy cream
Salt and pepper to taste

Place scallops and wine in frying pan; bring to boil. Lower heat and simmer for 2 to 3 minutes or until tender. Remove from heat; drain scallops; reserve liquid. Set scallops aside. Melt butter in saucepan. Stir in flour. Gradually stir in reserved liquid. Cook over low heat, stirring constantly, until thickened and smooth. Stir in cream and scallops. Heat to serving temperature. Remove from heat. Season with salt and pepper. Serves 3 to 4.

CAPTAIN KIDD'S SCALLOP SAUTÉ

2 pounds scallops
Cold milk
1 stick butter
Salt and pepper to taste
Flour mixed with favorite seasonings
Chives, minced
Lemon wedges

Season scallops with salt and pepper. Place scallops in a bowl; cover with cold milk and marinate for several minutes. Remove scallops; coat with seasoned flour. In large frying pan, melt 1 stick of butter and sauté scallops until golden brown. Remove from pan, sprinkle with chives and garnish with lemon wedges. Serves 6.

WRIGHT BROTHERS BROILED SCALLOPS

2 T. olive oil
1-1/2 pounds scallops
1/2 cup French dressing
1-1/2 cups bread crumbs
Favorite dipping sauce

Preheat broiler. Line broiling pan with aluminum foil; brush foil with oil. Dip scallops in French dressing; roll in crumbs. Arrange scallops on pan. Broil 4" from heat for 5 minutes on each side or until golden brown. Serve with favorite sauce. Serves 4.

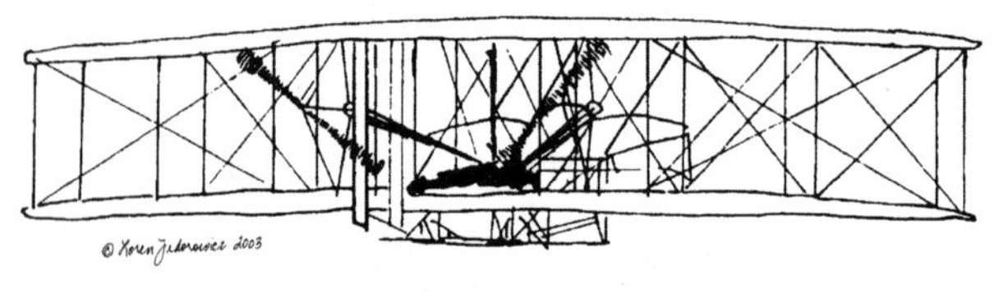

On Thursday, December 17, 1903 at 10:35 A.M., Orville Wright, piloting the Wright Flyer flew straight into a 47 mph wind. With Wilbur cheering on the ground, Orville guided the Flyer through the air for 12 seconds and landed 40 yards from where he took off. This image, now world famous was the only photograph that surf man John Daniels, from Kitty Hawk Lifesaving Station, ever took in his life.

RED DRUM

1-1/2 – 2 pounds fresh red drum fillets
1 tsp. salt
Pepper to taste
1 tsp. paprika
2 T. fresh lemon juice
2 tsp. onion, finely chopped
1/4 cup butter, melted

Preheat oven to 350° F. Place fish in lightly buttered baking dish, skin side down. Combine remaining ingredients in a separate bowl; pour over fillets. Bake uncovered for 20 to 25 minutes. Fish will be opaque and flake easily when done. Serves 4 to 6.

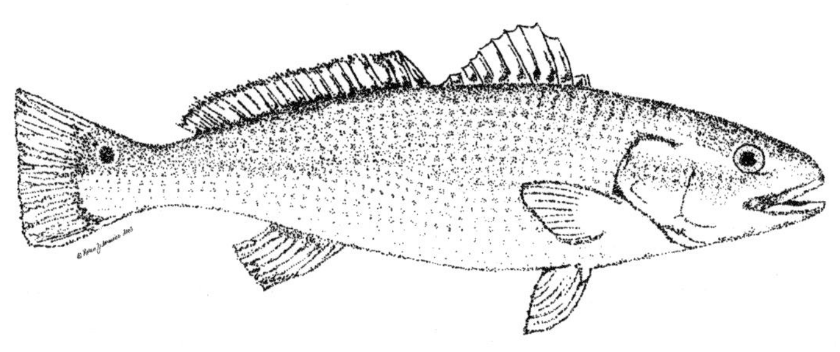

The bright Red Drum fish, also know as the Channel Bass or Redfish is easily recognizable because of its vivid reddish tones and distinctive black spot at the base of the tail. At full maturity the Red Drum can easily reach four feet in length and weigh in excess of forty pounds. The Red Drum is a popular sport fish, not only because it is eye-catching and readily sighted, but also because it is conveniently found in two locations. During incoming tides, the Red Drum swim into the shallow water of the tidal flat where food is the most abundant. They hunt for and dine on mollusks, crustaceans and mullet in the tidal grass. During outgoing tides, they move into deeper waters so they do not become trapped on the exposed tidal flat.

BALD HEAD BROILED FLOUNDER

2 large flounder
1/2 lemon, thinly sliced
1 stick butter, melted
Salt and pepper to taste
Juice of 1 lemon
1 T. fresh parsley, minced
3 green onions, diced

Score flounder with diagonal slits; place lemon slices into slits. In a saucepan, melt butter; add salt, pepper, lemon juice, parsley and onions. Broil flounder 4" to 5" from the heating element, for approximately 20 minutes, basting with sauce. Flounder should be moist and flake easily with a fork. Serves 2 to 3.

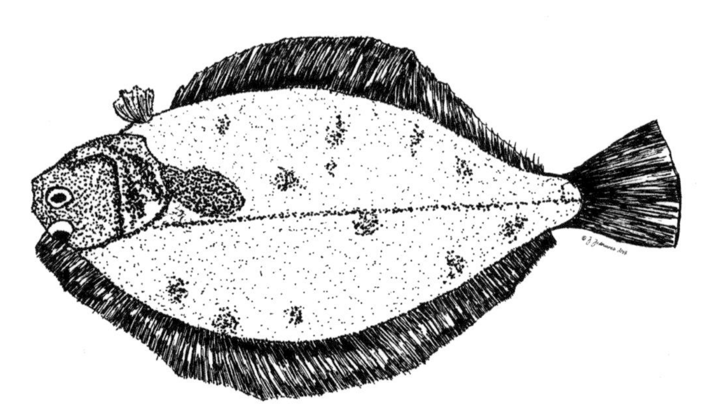

The Flounder fish lives a very interesting life. These fish go through an incredible transformation from birth to adulthood. They appear as normal fish as juveniles, but then transform into a flat, bottom-dwelling adult fish that is very well camouflaged and have both eyes on one side of their head! Summer Flounder, nicknamed "fluke," have both eyes on the left side of their head, whereas Winter Flounder have both of their eyes on the right side of their head. These fish can be a few inches to several feet in length and are important economically for their delicate meat.

CAPTAIN DAVE'S SENSATIONAL FLOUNDER FILLETS

4 medium-sized flounder fillets
2 sleeves of Ritz-style crackers, crushed
1/2 stick of butter, melted
1 clove garlic, minced
1/4 cup white wine
Juice of 1/2 lemon
1/2 tsp. dill weed
Salt to taste
Parsley flakes
Bread crumbs

Preheat oven to 350° F. In a medium bowl, add garlic to melted butter. Stir in lemon juice, white wine, parsley, dill and cracker crumbs. Mix well. Form mixture into a ball. Divide the ball into four equal parts for the four fillets. Roll each fillet around a portion of cracker ball. Place the stuffed fillet seam side down in a greased casserole dish. Place a pat of butter on each fillet and sprinkle with bread crumbs and parsley. Bake for 30 minutes or until fish is opaque and flakes easily with a fork. Serves 4.

STEAMED CLAMS

2 quarts unshucked soft-shell clams *Melted butter*

Scrub clams thoroughly. Place in large kettle with 1/2 inch water in bottom. Cover tightly. Cook over high heat for 6 to 10 minutes from the time water begins to boil rapidly; or until clams open. Discard clams that do not open. Serve in soup plates with a bowl of melted butter for dipping. Serves 2.

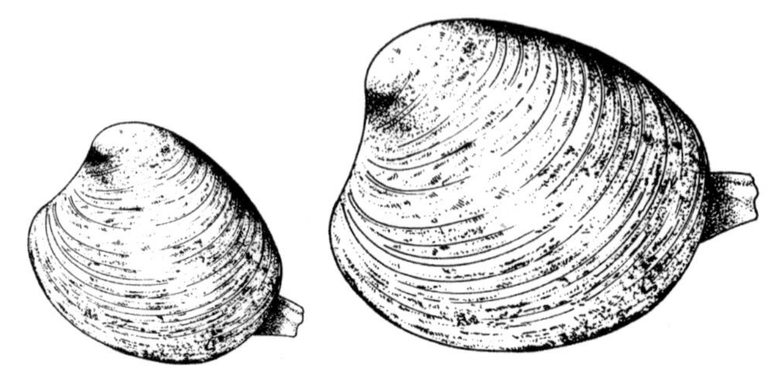

The Clam, a type of Mollusk, is a well-known food delicacy along the East coast. These rather sedentary creatures, encased in a hard grayish shell, spend their lives buried in mud or sand usually along the shore or in shallow waters. They are considered "filter feeders," which means they feed on small organisms and debris that float around in the water by siphoning in water over their gills. In some parts of the world, the adults can weigh up to 440 lbs., span 3.3 feet across and are brilliantly colored in vibrant blues, greens and reds. These larger clams mainly live in slightly deeper water resting on top of the ocean floor rather than burying themselves.

STUFFED QUAHOGS

5 large quahogs, save shells
1 medium onion, quartered
1/4 tsp. salt
Dash of pepper
1/2 tsp. oregano
1 cup fresh bread crumbs
2 T. butter

Preheat oven to 400° F. Shuck quahogs, remove meat, reserve the liquid, and reserve shells. Clean and dry shells; set aside. Place the quahog meat and onion in a food processor and process to medium consistency and well blended. Or use a meat grinder with a medium blade and save the liquid. Combine ground mixture, reserved liquid, salt, pepper, oregano and bread crumbs. Spoon ground mixture into reserved shells. Place on baking sheet. Dot with butter. Bake for 20 minutes. Serves 5.

HATTERAS J'S SPANISH MACKEREL

Extra Virgin Olive Oil
2 pounds Spanish Mackerel (fillets)
1 medium sweet onion, sliced
1 cup chopped fresh tomato or
1 can diced tomato, drained
2 tsp. salt
1/2 tsp. pepper

Preheat oven to 375° F. Brush a shallow baking pan with olive oil. Place fish in dish; drizzle olive oil over fish and rub; this will keep the fish from getting too dry. Sprinkle with salt and pepper. Arrange onion slice on top; pour tomatoes over all. Bake uncovered for 30 minutes or until fish flakes easily with a fork. Serves 4.

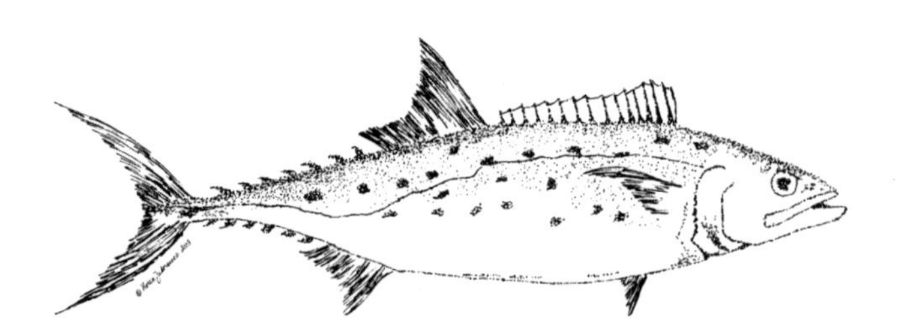

A colorful fish, the Spanish mackerel is marked by a vibrant blue-green back, accentuated by large, oval-shaped orange-yellow spots peppered along its white sides. This fish is very feisty and fast, making it a popular fish among sport fishermen. Inhabiting the warmer waters of both the inshore and offshore regions, the Spanish mackerel prefers traveling in large schools for protection from predators. These large schools are amazingly discernable from the air.

ALLIGATOR RIVER GRILLED SEAFOOD STEAKS

Favorite fish

1 cup favorite bottled Italian dressing

Place fish in shallow dish and pour salad dressing over steaks, coating both sides well. Cover with plastic wrap and marinate in the refrigerator for 1 hour. Place fish on clean, preheated and oiled grill. Grill fish until opaque and flakes easily, basting frequently with Italian dressing.

Extremely fast swimmers, the Atlantic Sailfish has the ability to swim at amazing speeds of 60 mph. Along with its prominent feature of its sail-like blue-spotted dorsal fin, the coloration of the Sailfish begins with dark blue on their back which gradually fades to silver-white underneath. The Sailfish seeks either the Gulf Stream current, or the warmer currents adjoining the continental shelf, where the water temperature remains between 70°F and 85° F. Unfortunately, because of its legendary reputation as fast swimmers and dramatic leapers out of the water, this highly popular game fish among sport fishermen is noticeably declining due to excessive over fishing.

MANTEO MARINATED FILLETS

2 pounds fresh fish fillets
1/3 cup oil
3 T. soy sauce
2 T. wine vinegar
2 T. onion, finely chopped
1 clove garlic, minced

Place fish in a glass baking dish or a re-sealable plastic bag. Combine oil, soy sauce, vinegar, onion and garlic. Mix well. Pour the mixture over fish and marinate in the refrigerator for 30 to 60 minutes turning occasionally. Remove the fish, saving the marinade. Preheat both sides of grill on high for 10 minutes. Place fish on well-oiled grill to prevent sticking. Close hood and cook approximately 15 minutes or until fish is done, turning once. Brush fish occasionally with marinade. Fish is done when it is opaque and flakes easily with a fork. Serves 6.

FISH IN A BASKET

4 fillets of favorite white fish
1/2 cup flour
1/2 tsp. salt
1/4 tsp. pepper
1/4 cup butter, melted

In bowl combine flour, salt, and pepper. Dip fish in flour mixture, coating thoroughly. Place coated fish in well-oiled grill basket. Preheat both sides of grill on high for 10 minutes. Place basket on grill. Close hood and cook for approximately 20 minutes, turning once and basting often with butter. Serves 4.

FAVORITE FISH PARMESANO

Breaded fish fillets
1 cup favorite spaghetti sauce
1/2 cup grated mozzarella
2 T. grated Parmesan cheese

Preheat oven to 375° F. Pour spaghetti sauce in greased, shallow baking dish. Place fish on top of sauce and cover with grated mozzarella cheese. Sprinkle with parmesan cheese and bake uncovered for 20 minutes.

MARITIME BAKED FISH

2 pounds of favorite fish fillets
2-1/2 cups seasoned bread crumbs
2/3 cups fresh mushrooms, sliced
1/2 cup butter, melted
1-1/2 cans (12 oz.) evaporated milk

Preheat oven at 350° F. Grease bottom of 4-quart casserole dish. Sprinkle bottom with light coating of bread crumbs. Cut fish into serving size pieces and place half of the fish in the bottom of the casserole dish. Mix the remaining bread crumbs, mushrooms and melted butter together and spread 1/2 the mixture on top of the fish. Add the rest of the fish and top with the remaining bread crumb mixture. Slowly pour the evaporated milk over all and bake for 30 minutes. Serves 4.

WAVES BAKED FISH DELIGHT

2 pounds flounder or white fish fillets
1/2 cup crab meat, flaked
1/2 cup shrimp, chopped
1 can cheddar cheese soup, undiluted
3 T. mushrooms, chopped
3 T. green onion, chopped
1/4 tsp. salt
1/2 tsp. dried tarragon
1 clove garlic, minced
Butter
1/2 cup milk
1 T. fresh tarragon, chopped fine
2 T. green onion, sliced thin for garnish

Preheat oven to 375° F. Place half the fish fillets in a buttered baking dish. Combine 1/4 cup of soup with crab, shrimp, mushrooms, green onion, salt, dried tarragon and garlic. Spread mixture over fillets. Cover with remaining fillets and dot with butter. Bake uncovered for 30 minutes or until fish flakes easily with a fork. Take remaining soup, combine with milk, onion and fresh tarragon. Heat over low heat until warm. Pour over fish when ready to serve. Serves 4.

CASTAWAY BAKED FISH

1-1/2 pounds fish fillets
3/4 tsp. salt
Pepper to taste
2 T. butter, melted
1 T. flour
1 cup hot water
1 T. fresh lemon juice
1 T. mustard
1/2 cup bread crumbs

Preheat oven to 400° F. Season fillets with salt and pepper; place in shallow, greased baking pan. In a separate bowl, melt 1 tablespoon butter and blend with flour. Add hot water, lemon juice and mustard. Stir frequently until thickened. Pour over fish. Add remaining tablespoon of butter to bread crumbs, mix, and sprinkle over fish. Bake uncovered for 20 minutes. Serves 4.

GULL SHOALS BAKED FISH

2 pounds fish fillets
3 T. fresh lemon juice
1/3 cup bread crumbs
1/2 cup green olives, chopped
2 tsp. oregano
1 garlic clove, minced
1/4 tsp. white pepper
Lemon wedges

Preheat oven to 450° F. Place in greased 9"x13" baking pan. Mix lemon juice, bread crumbs, olives, oregano, garlic and white pepper together. Spread mixture over fish fillets cover and bake for 10 to 12 minutes or until fish flakes easily. Garnish with lemon wedges. Serves 4.

WHITE CLAM SAUCE WITH ANGEL HAIR PASTA

1/4 cup olive oil
1/2 cup butter
3 cloves of garlic, chopped
3 cans of minced clams, undrained
1 tsp. white pepper
3 T. fresh basil, finely chopped
3 T. fresh parsley, finely chopped
1 pound angel hair pasta

Cook pasta according to directions; drain; do not rinse. In a medium saucepan, melt butter and oil together; sauté garlic. When garlic is slightly browned, add clams with juice, pepper and basil. Cover and simmer for 10 minutes. Place pasta in large serving bowl. Pour clam sauce over pasta; toss and serve. Garnish with chopped parsley. Serves 4.

SALVO SEAFOOD LASAGNA

8 oz. pkg. cream cheese
1 pint ricotta cheese
1 T. basil, chopped fine
1/2 pound crabmeat
1/2 pound shrimp
2 cans cream of shrimp soup, undiluted
1 medium onion, chopped
1 egg, beaten
Salt and pepper to taste
1 pkg. lasagna noodles, cooked and drained
1 cup cheddar cheese, grated

Cook lasagna noodles according to package directions; drain. Cream together cream cheese, ricotta and basil; set aside. Preheat oven to 350° F. Grease a 9"x13" baking dish. In a large bowl, mix crabmeat, onion and egg. Add soup to mixture; mix until well blended. Place a layer of cooked lasagna noodles in prepared baking dish. Spoon a layer of the cream cheese mixture over the noodles followed by the seafood mix on top of the cheese mixture. Repeat. Cover with foil and bake 30 to 45 minutes or until thoroughly heated. Remove foil, sprinkle with cheddar cheese; return to oven to melt cheese. Serves 6.

CASSEROLES
SIDES
VEGETABLES

Old Baldy or Bald Head Island Lighthouse was built on Smith Island in 1817. Built to serve as an important marker for ships navigating the Cape Fear River Channel, the Bald Head Island Lighthouse was retired in 1958 after Oak Island came into service. Still serving as a day marker for ships, this octagonal-shaped lighthouse is still guarding its sandy, barren beaches and is the oldest lighthouse in North Carolina.

BUXTON BAKED FISH CASSEROLE

2 pounds fresh fish
1/2 cup onion, sliced
1/4 cup butter
Salt and pepper to taste
1-1/2 cups bread crumbs
1/2 cup parmesan cheese
3/4 cup milk

Preheat oven to 350° F. Cut fish into serving size pieces, sprinkle with salt and pepper; set aside. In a separate pan; melt butter; sauté onion until transparent; add salt, pepper, breadcrumbs and cheese; toss lightly. In a greased baking dish, alternate layers of fish and bread crumb topping beginning with a layer of fish and finishing with the bread crumb layer on top. Slowly pour milk over the top; bake uncovered for 45 minutes. Serves 6.

BAKED SEAFOOD CASSEROLE

1 cup cooked crabmeat, flaked
1 cup cooked shrimp, de-veined and peeled
3 T. green pepper, chopped
1 medium onion, chopped
3/4 tsp. salt
Dash of pepper
1 tsp. Worcestershire sauce
1/2 tsp. dry mustard
3/4 cup mayonnaise
1 cup bread crumbs
2 T. butter

Preheat oven to 350° F. Combine all of the ingredients except for half the bread crumbs and butter. Place in a greased 9"x13" baking dish. Melt the 2 tablespoons of butter and add to remaining bread crumbs, tossing lightly with a fork. Add buttered crumbs on top of casserole and bake uncovered for 30 minutes. Serves 6.

FISH AU GRATIN

2 cups cooked tuna or crab, flaked
2 T. butter
2 T. flour
1/2 tsp. salt
2 cups milk
3/4 cup Swiss cheese, grated
1 T. Worcestershire sauce
1/2 cup buttered bread crumbs

Preheat oven to 350° F. Melt butter in saucepan over medium heat; add flour and salt. Cook, stirring frequently, until flour is light and bubbly, but not brown; about 3 minutes. Reduce heat and gradually stir in milk; cook until thickened, about 8 to10 minutes. Add cheese and cook until melted. Stir in Worcestershire sauce and flaked fish. Place into greased baking dish and sprinkle with buttered breadcrumbs. Bake uncovered for 25 minutes or until golden brown. Serves 6.

ZUCCHINI CHEESE CASSEROLE

3 cups zucchini, shredded
1 cup pizza crust mix
1/2 cup onion, chopped
4 eggs
1 cup Swiss cheese, grated
1/4 cup milk
1/2 tsp. salt
1/2 tsp. seasoned salt
1 T. fresh parsley, finely chopped
1 T. fresh oregano, finely chopped
1/4 tsp. pepper

Preheat oven to 350° F. Mix all ingredients in a large bowl and pour into greased 8" square pan. Bake uncovered for 30 minutes.

CRAB CASSEROLE

1 cup cooked crabmeat
3 T. butter
2 small onions, chopped
1 green pepper, chopped
3 stalks celery, chopped
1 large can evaporated milk
1 tsp. salt
1 tsp. paprika
1/3 cup mayonnaise
1-1/2 cup seashell macaroni, cooked and drained

Preheat oven to 375° F. Sauté vegetables in butter until tender. Add seasonings, mayonnaise and milk. Stir in crab and macaroni. Place in a greased baking dish and bake covered for 30 minutes. Serves 3 to 4.

CAROLINA TOO DEVILED CRAB

2 pounds fresh lump crab meat
2 cups Cream Sauce*, see page 21*
1 tsp. dry mustard
Juice of 1/2 lemon
1/4 cup sherry
1/4 cup chives, chopped
3 eggs, hard cooked, chopped
Bread crumbs
Paprika
Butter

Preheat oven to 450° F. Grease 6 crab shells or 2-quart casserole dish. Combine crab meat and Cream Sauce. Stir in mustard, lemon juice, sherry, chives and eggs. Fill shells or casserole. Sprinkle with crumbs. Garnish with paprika; dot with butter. Bake for 15 minutes, or until lightly browned. Serves 6.

SWANQUARTER SHRIMP AND CRAB BAKE

1/2 pound cooked shrimp, coarsely chopped
1/2 pound cooked crabmeat, flaked
1 green pepper, chopped
1 medium onion, chopped
1 cup celery, chopped
1/2 tsp. salt
Dash of pepper
1 tsp. Worcestershire sauce
1 cup mayonnaise
1 cup seasoned bread crumbs

Preheat oven to 350° F. In a large mixing bowl, gently combine all ingredients, except bread crumbs. Place mixture in greased casserole dish; dot with butter; sprinkle with bread crumbs. Bake uncovered for 30 minutes or until hot and bubbly. Serves 8.

KITTY HAWK CRAB CASSEROLE

2 cups White Sauce, see page 20
1 tsp. salt
1/8 tsp. pepper
1/2 tsp. celery salt
Dash of cayenne
1 egg yolk, lightly beaten
2 T. dry sherry
2 cups crab meat, flaked
1 cup fresh bread crumbs
1 T. parsley, chopped
1 T. onion, finely chopped
3 T. melted butter
Paprika

Preheat oven to 400° F. Grease 1-1/2 quart casserole. Place White Sauce in large saucepan. Stir in salt, pepper, celery salt, cayenne and egg yolk. Cook over medium heat, stirring constantly until hot. Remove from heat. Stir in sherry; mix until smooth. Add crab meat, 1/2 cup of the bread crumbs, parsley and onion; mix well. Pour into casserole. Combine remaining crumbs and butter; sprinkle over casserole. Sprinkle with paprika. Bake uncovered for 20 minutes, or until browned. Serves 4 to 6.

BAKED CRAB CASSEROLE

1 pound cooked crab meat, flaked
4 T. roasted red pepper, diced
3 T. green pepper, finely chopped
2 T. prepared mustard
1 tsp. Worcestershire
1 tsp. salt
1 egg, lightly beaten
1/2 cup bread crumbs
2 T. milk
1 cup mayonnaise
2 egg yolks, beaten

Preheat oven to 375° F. Grease 1-1/2 quart casserole. In mixing bowl combine all ingredients except mayonnaise and egg yolks; mix well. Spoon into casserole. In small bowl, mix mayonnaise and egg yolks. Spread over crab mixture. Bake uncovered for 25 minutes, or until golden brown. Serves 4.

CALICO JACK'S CRABMEAT AND MUSHROOMS

1 pound fresh lump crab meat
1/4 cup butter
1/4 pound fresh mushrooms, sliced
2 T. flour
1/2 cup milk
1/2 cup dry white wine
1/4 tsp. dry mustard
1/4 tsp. tarragon
1/2 tsp. salt
1/8 tsp. pepper
1/2 cup bread crumbs

Preheat oven to 350° F. Grease 4 individual casserole dishes. Flake crab meat; set aside. Melt butter in saucepan; sauté mushrooms for 5 minutes. Stir in flour. Gradually stir in milk and wine. Cook over low heat, stirring constantly, until thickened and smooth. Add mustard, tarragon, salt, pepper and crab meat. Simmer for 2 minutes. Spoon into casserole dishes. Sprinkle with bread crumbs. Bake for 30 minutes. Serves 4.

AVON CRAB MEAT CASSEROLE

2-1/2 cups White Sauce, *see page 20*
2 - 6-1/2 oz. cans crab meat, drained and flaked
2 - 4 oz. cans of sliced mushroom, drained
1/2 cup green pepper, finely chopped
4 T. pimientos, diced
1/2 cup slivered almonds
4 eggs, hard cooked and chopped
2 tsp. fresh lemon juice
1 cup Cheddar cheese, shredded
1/2 cup buttered bread crumbs
Salt and pepper to taste

Preheat oven to 350° F. Grease 2 quart casserole. Pour White Sauce into a large mixing bowl; season with salt and pepper. Gently stir in all remaining ingredients except cheese and crumbs; toss lightly, spoon into casserole dish. Sprinkle with cheese and bread crumbs. Bake uncovered for 45 minutes. Serves 8.

SANDY BAY SHRIMP CASSEROLE

2-1/2 cups canned artichoke hearts
1 pound cooked shrimp, peeled, de-veined
2 T. butter
1/4 pound fresh mushrooms, sliced
1 T. Worcestershire
1/4 cup dry sherry
1-1/2 cups White Sauce *(see page 20)*
1/4 cup grated Parmesan cheese
Paprika
Parsley

Preheat oven to 375° F. Grease 2 quart casserole dish. Arrange artichokes in casserole dish. Layer shrimp over artichokes. Melt butter in frying pan; sauté mushrooms for 5 minutes. Pour over shrimp. In a separate bowl, combine Worcestershire, sherry and White Sauce. Pour over artichokes and shrimp. Sprinkle with Parmesan cheese and paprika. Bake for 30 to 40 minutes. Garnish with parsley before serving. Serves 4.

PINE ISLAND SHRIMP TETRAZZINI

2 T. butter
1/2 pound fresh mushrooms, sliced
1/2 pound spaghetti, cooked
1 pound cooked shrimp
2 cans cream of mushroom soup, undiluted
1/2 cup light cream
2 T. sherry
1/3 cup grated Parmesan cheese

Preheat oven to 375° F. Grease 1-1/2 quart casserole dish. Peel and de-vein shrimp; set aside. Melt butter in saucepan; sauté mushrooms until tender. Add spaghetti, shrimp, soup, cream and sherry. Spoon into casserole dish. Sprinkle with cheese. Bake for 30 minutes. If necessary, place under broiler to brown top. Serves 4.

BODIE ISLAND TUNA NOODLE CASSEROLE

2 cups medium wide, cooked noodles
1 can cream of mushroom soup, undiluted
1/2 cup milk
1 - 7 oz. can tuna, drained and flaked
1 cup Cheddar cheese, shredded
1/3 cup onion, finely chopped
1/2 cup crushed potato chips
Paprika

Preheat oven to 425° F. Grease 1-1/2 quart casserole dish. Cook noodles according to package directions; drain, do not rinse. In a medium mixing bowl, combine soup, milk, tuna, cheese and onion. Add noodles; mix well and pour into casserole dish. Sprinkle with potato chips and paprika. Bake for 15 minutes, or until bubbling. Serves 4.

BAKED CLAMS AU GRATIN

2 cups clams, finely chopped
3 slices bacon, diced
1/4 cup butter
1/2 cup celery, finely chopped
1/2 cup green pepper, finely chopped
1/2 cup onions, finely chopped
3 T. flour
2 cups milk
1 tsp. salt
1/4 tsp. pepper
1 cup Cheddar cheese, grated
2 eggs, lightly beaten

Preheat oven to 350° F. Grease 2 quart casserole dish. Cook bacon over medium heat in a saucepan until crisp. Lower heat and add butter and cook for 3 minutes. Add celery, green pepper and onions and sauté for 5 minutes. Blend in flour. Gradually stir in milk. Cook over low heat, stirring constantly, until thickened and smooth. Remove from heat. Stir in salt, pepper, 1/2 cup of the cheese, eggs and clams. Pour into casserole dish. Sprinkle with remaining cheese. Bake for 25 minutes or until golden and bubbling. Serves 4.

Sea horses, found in temperate waters, are actually fish that come in many different sizes and beautiful colors. Sea horses have the ability to hide from their enemies by changing their color to blend in with their surrounding environment. Unlike most fish that swim on their stomach, the Sea horse swims very slowly, standing up. When they are not swimming, the Sea horse spends much of its time standing very still with their long, strong tails wrapped around sea grass or coral.

BAKED OYSTERS HATTERAS

6 large, cleaned scallop or clam shells
24 freshly shucked oysters with liquid
2 T. butter
2 medium green peppers, diced
4 medium fresh mushrooms, diced
1 cup hot WHITE SAUCE – see page 20
1 egg yolk
Salt and pepper to taste
1 T. heavy cream
1/4 pound fresh lump crab meat, flaked
1/2 cup grated Parmesan cheese

Preheat oven to 450° F. Place oysters in saucepan with 1/2 inch of water. Bring to boil. Remove from heat. Remove and discard hard muscle from each oyster. Arrange 4 oysters in each of 6 scallop or clam shells. Set aside. Melt butter in medium saucepan; cook mushrooms and green peppers over low heat for 10 minutes, or until peppers are tender but not browned. In a separate bowl, combine White Sauce, egg yolk, salt and pepper; blend in whipping cream. Combine sauce, vegetables and crab meat. Spoon over oysters. Sprinkle with cheese. Bake for 10 minutes or until sauce is bubbling and cheese is browned. Serves 6.

KNOTTS ISLAND SCALLOPS BAKED IN CREAM

2 pounds scallops
1 cup cracker crumbs
1-1/2 tsp. salt
1/4 tsp. pepper
1/2 tsp. basil
1/2 tsp. oregano
1 T. parsley, finely chopped
1 cup heavy cream

Preheat oven to 375° F. Butter 9"x13" baking pan. In a separate baking dish, combine crumbs, salt, pepper, basil, oregano and parsley. Coat scallops; arrange in the prepared baking dish. Pour cream over scallops. Bake, uncovered for 25 minutes, or until bubbling and lightly browned. Serves 4.

BAKED SEAFOOD SALAD

6 T. green pepper, chopped
3 T. onion, chopped
1 cup celery, chopped
1 cup mayonnaise
1 cup cooked crab meat, flaked
1 cup cooked shrimp
1/2 tsp. salt
1/4 tsp. pepper
1/2 tsp. Worcestershire sauce
3/4 cup potato chips, crushed

Preheat oven to 350° F. Peel, de-vein and chop shrimp; set aside. Mix all of the ingredients together except the potato chips. Spoon mixture into a greased 9"x13" baking dish. Sprinkle crushed potato chips over top and bake for 30 minutes. Serves 3 to 4.

NAGS HEAD TUNA CASSEROLE

1 pound spaghetti
1 stick butter
4 T. flour
1/2 tsp. salt
1/2 tsp. celery salt
1/4 tsp. paprika
1/2 tsp. black pepper
2 cups milk
1-1/2 cup American cheese, shredded
2 - 7oz. cans tuna
1 cup bread crumbs

Preheat oven to 350° F. Cook spaghetti according to directions. Drain; do not rinse. Melt 6 tablespoons butter in a saucepan over medium heat; add flour; mix well. Cook 3–4 minutes until flour is light and bubbly; add seasonings, blending well. Lower heat; stir in milk a little at a time until thickened. Add 1 cup cheese; stir until melted. Stir in cooked pasta and tuna. Pour into greased baking dish. Melt remaining 2 tablespoons butter; add bread crumbs and remaining cheese tossing lightly. Spoon over casserole. Bake uncovered for 30 to 35 minutes or until golden brown. Serves 4.

CRAB NOODLE BAKE

2 T. butter
1 onion, chopped
1/2 cup fresh mushrooms, sliced
1 green pepper, chopped
8 oz. pkg. medium noodles, cooked
1-1/2 cups crabmeat, flaked
2-1/2 cups canned tomatoes, drained
1 cup sour cream

Cook noodles per package instructions; drain. Do not rinse. Preheat oven to 350° F. Grease 2-1/2 quart casserole dish. Melt butter in a medium saucepan; sauté onions until transparent; add mushrooms and green pepper; cook until vegetables are tender. Combine vegetables, noodles, crabmeat and tomatoes. Pour into casserole dish; spread sour cream on top. Bake uncovered for 45 minutes. Serves 4.

LOREN'S CHEESY SHRIMP CASSEROLE

6 slices day old bread
1/2 pound small fresh shrimp
1 cup Cheddar cheese, shredded
4 eggs, beaten
2 cups milk
1 tsp. fresh lemon juice
1/2 tsp. salt
1/4 tsp. pepper
1/4 tsp. dill weed

Preheat oven to 350° F. Peel and de-vein shrimp; set aside. Butter a 2 quart casserole dish. Trim bread slices. Butter both sides of 3 slices of bread and place in bottom of casserole. Place shrimp on top of bread. Sprinkle cheese over the shrimp. Butter the remaining bread; place on top of shrimp and cheese. Beat eggs; add milk and remaining ingredients. Pour over bread and shrimp. Cover with plastic wrap and refrigerate for 1 hour or more so the egg mixture can be absorbed. Place casserole in a large baking pan and add 1" of hot water to create a water bath. This will prevent the casserole from getting too brown on the bottom. Bake uncovered for 45 minutes. Serves 2.

RUNBOAT RICE FLORENTINE

3 cups cooked rice
1/4 cup butter
4 eggs, lightly beaten
1 pound sharp Cheddar cheese, shredded
1 cup milk
1 T. Worcestershire
1 tsp. marjoram
1 tsp. thyme
10 oz. pkg. frozen chopped spinach, cooked and drained
1 T. onion, chopped
2 tsp. salt

Preheat oven to 350° F. Grease 2-quart casserole dish. Melt butter in saucepan. Over medium heat, stir in eggs, cheese, milk, spinach and onion cook, stirring constantly, until cheese is melted. Remove from heat and add remaining ingredients. Pour into casserole dish, cover and bake for 35 minutes. Serves 8.

ZUCCHINI CASSEROLE

6 cups zucchini, grated (do not peel)
1 medium onion, chopped
1 can mushroom soup
1 carrot, grated
1 cup sour cream
8 oz. pkg. seasoned stuffing mix
1/4 cup butter

Preheat oven at 350°F. Grease 3 quart casserole dish. Cook onion and zucchini together for 5 minutes; drain and set aside. Mix mushroom soup, grated onion and sour cream. Fold into zucchini and onion mixture; set aside. Combine stuffing with 1/4 cup butter; put 1/2 of stuffing mix into a casserole dish. Add zucchini mixture; top with remaining stuffing. Bake uncovered for 35 minutes. Serves 4–6.

HEARTY HEFTY ZUCCHINI CASSEROLE

6 cups zucchini, grated
1 medium onion, chopped
1 can mushroom soup
1 carrot, grated
1 cup sour cream
8 oz. pkg. seasoned stuffing mix
1/4 cup butter, melted
1 pound pork sausage

Preheat oven to 350° F. Grease a 4 quart casserole dish. Cook sausage, crumbling as it cooks; drain; set aside. In a large pan cook onion and zucchini together for 5 minutes; drain. In a separate bowl, mix mushroom soup, grated carrot and sour cream. Fold into zucchini mixture; add cooked sausage. Mix melted butter and stuffing mix in separate bowl. Spoon 1/2 the stuffing into casserole dish; add the vegetable-meat mixture; top with remaining stuffing. Bake for 35 minutes. Serves 4–6.

CAPTAIN BEARD'S SCALLOPS SUPREME

2 pounds scallops
1/2 cup butter, melted
1 clove garlic, minced
2 sleeves Ritz-style crackers, crushed
Juice of half a lemon
1/4 cup white wine
1/2 tsp. dill weed
1 T. parsley, chopped
1 tsp. salt
1/2 tsp. pepper

Preheat oven to 350° F. Grease a 4 quart casserole dish. Drain scallops; dry with paper toweling. Crush crackers with a rolling pin; set aside. Add garlic to melted butter in a medium sized mixing bowl. Mix in white wine, lemon juice, parsley, dill weed, salt, pepper and cracker crumbs. Gently mix ingredients together to resemble coarse crumbs. Spread a layer of the cracker crumbs in the bottom of the casserole dish followed by a layer of scallops. Repeat the process ending with a layer of cracker crumbs. Bake uncovered for approximately 45 minutes. Check the bottom layer of scallops for doneness. Scallops will be opaque and fork tender when cooked. Serves 8.

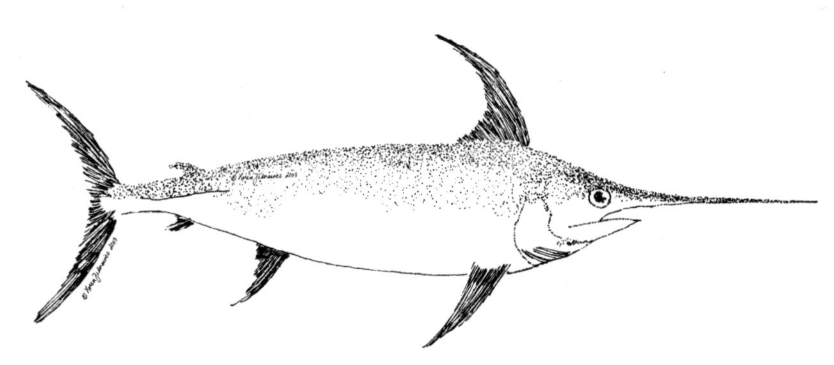

The Blue marlin is often considered the most highly sought after game fish because of its incredible strength, stamina, speed and spectacular leaps. The beautiful grey-blue to dark-blue sides highlighted with purplish bands and silver-white belly and sides actually accentuate the Blue marlin's long spear-like upper jaw and two dorsal fins. Inhabiting temperate waters, the blue marlin can be found gracefully migrating along the current waters next to the edge of the continental shelf. Although considered high quality meat, the Blue marlin is predominately a recreational sport fish in North America and therefore, the fish is more often caught and released, rather than consumed.

NANNY'S CUCUMBERS

3 large cucumbers, peeled and thinly sliced
1 cup white sugar
1/2 cup vinegar (white or cider)
Chopped green and/or red pepper for color (optional)
Thinly sliced onion or scallions to taste
Few shakes of celery salt

Salt cucumbers lightly and set aside for 5 to15 minutes. Rinse and drain. Mix vinegar and sugar together, add cucumbers, onions and celery salt to liquid and let it set for 12 hours in the refrigerator to blend flavors. For variety, drain liquid and add 1/2 cup or more sour cream and mix thoroughly.

CORN BREAD PUDDING

1 stick margarine, melted
1 can cream corn
1 pkg. corn muffin mix (8 oz.)
1 cup sour cream
1 can whole kernel corn

Preheat oven to 350° F. Mix all ingredients and pour into greased baking dish. Bake at 350° F for 30 minutes or until golden brown.

HUSH PUPPIES

Oil for frying

1 cup coarse yellow corn meal
1/2 cup all-purpose flour
1-1/2 tsp. baking powder
2/3 cups milk
3/4 tsp. salt
2 T. onion, minced
1 egg

Mix dry ingredients together. Beat egg, add milk and onion; stir into dry ingredients. Drop by teaspoonfuls into hot oil. Fry until golden brown and serve hot with fried fish.

ALBEMARLE FISH AND RICE

4 T. olive oil
1-1/2 cups rice, uncooked
3 cups boiling water
2 tsp. salt
1/4 cup butter
1 cup onions, chopped
1 clove garlic, crushed
4 fillets of favorite white fish, cut into 4-inch squares
1/2 tsp. pepper
1 T. fresh oregano, chopped fine
1 T. fresh basil, chopped fine
3 T. parsley, chopped
1 cup tomatoes, diced

Heat 2 tablespoons of the oil in saucepan; sauté rice over low heat, stirring frequently, until golden. Add water and salt; cover; cook over low heat for 15 minutes or until water is absorbed. Remove from heat; set aside. Heat remaining oil and butter together in large frying pan; sauté onions and garlic over medium heat until onions are transparent. Add fish, pepper, oregano and basil; cook for 10 minutes. Add rice, parsley and tomatoes; mix gently. Cook over low heat for 15 minutes, stirring frequently. Serves 4.

OUTER BANKS CLAMS AND RISOTTO

1/4 cup olive oil
1 onion, chopped finely
1 clove garlic, minced
2 cups tomatoes
8 oz. bottle clam juice
2 T. parsley, chopped
1 T. fresh basil, chopped
8 oz. can minced clams, undrained
1 cup rice, uncooked
3/4 tsp. salt
Fresh cherrystone or little neck clams, washed

Heat oil in medium saucepan; sauté onion and garlic for 5 minutes or until onion is transparent. Add tomatoes, clam juice, parsley, and basil. Bring to boil. Reduce heat; simmer for 30 minutes. Add minced clams; bring back to a boil. Stir in rice and salt; reduce heat. Arrange fresh clams on rice; cover; cook over low heat for 20 minutes, or until rice is cooked and clams have opened. Serves 4.

ROANOKE RIVER SHRIMP BOATS

1 cup cooked rice
1 large onion, chopped
1 cup heavy cream
1/2 cup catsup
1 cup cooked shrimp
Puff pastry shells, baked

Peel, de-vein and chop shrimp; set aside. In a heavy saucepan, sauté onion until transparent; add rice and cream. Cook over low heat for 15 minutes, stirring occasionally. Add catsup and shrimp; cook for 30 minutes longer. Serve in puff pastry shells. Serves 3.

PAMLICO SOUND SHRIMP NEUVO

2 pounds fresh shrimp
1 cup rice
1 cup water
2 slices bacon
1 medium onion, chopped
1 red pepper, chopped
2 T. melted butter
1 tsp. salt
1 tsp. Creole seasoning

Peel and de-vein shrimp; set aside. In a heavy saucepan, place rice, water and shrimp cut into bite sized pieces. Dice bacon and fry in a separate pan until crisp. Add onion and green pepper; sauté until onion is lightly browned; add to rice and shrimp mixture. Add butter, salt and Creole seasoning. Mix well. Cover; cook over low heat for 40 minutes or until tender. Serves 6.

SHRIMP SHARI

1 large can tomatoes
1/2 cup onions, chopped
1/2 cup celery, chopped
2 tsp. fresh lemon juice
2 tsp. salt
2 T. catsup
2 T. Worcestershire
2 T. butter
1 cup rice
1 pound shrimp, peeled and de-veined

In large saucepan combine tomatoes, onions and celery. Bring to boil; cover; simmer for 15 minutes. Add lemon juice, salt, catsup, Worcestershire and butter. Bring to boil; stir in rice, cover; simmer for 15 minutes. Stir in shrimp; cook uncovered for 15 minutes or until liquid is absorbed. Serves 4.

CANDY'S BAKED PINEAPPLE

3 cups day old bread, cubed
1 stick butter, melted
1/2 cup sugar
3 eggs, beaten
1 - 20 oz. can crushed pineapple, drained

Preheat oven to 350° F. Toss all ingredients together and place in buttered 1-1/2 quart casserole dish. Bake uncovered at 350°F for 40 minutes.

POTATO PANCAKES

Oil for frying

6 large baking potatoes, grated
1 medium onion, grated
1/4 cup milk
1/4 cup flour
2 large eggs, beaten
Salt and pepper

In a large mixing bowl, grate potatoes, stir in milk (milk keeps the potatoes from discoloring), add grated onion; mix together. Add eggs, flour, salt and pepper. Mix well. Heat a generous amount of oil in a large frying pan or a griddle. Spoon potato batter onto cooking surface and flatten with the back of the spoon. Fry until crisp and browned on one side before turning. Serve with sour cream or applesauce.

FRYING PAN SHOALS ROASTED POTATOES

4 large baking potatoes
Olive oil
Salt and pepper to taste
1 T. fresh rosemary, finely chopped
1 T. fresh thyme, finely chopped

Preheat oven to 400° F. Scrub potatoes; cut potatoes in half lengthwise into thin wedges and brush each side with oil. Lay the potato wedges on a greased baking pan in a single layer. Sprinkle potatoes with salt, pepper and herbs. Bake for 20 minutes or until golden and crispy.

KILL DEVIL HILLS CHARGRILLED VEGETABLES

2 red bell peppers, quartered
4 medium zucchini
1 large sweet onion, quartered
2 large sweet potatoes
Olive oil

Peel and cut the sweet potatoes into wedges and boil until barely tender; drain. Cut zucchini in half lengthwise and then in half to quarter. Sprinkle zucchini with a little salt and let it sit for 15 minutes; pat dry. Toss peppers, zucchini, onion and potato wedges with olive oil in a large bowl making sure the vegetables are coated. Cook on a clean preheated grill until slightly charred and soft. Serve hot.

HONEY GLAZED CARROTS

1 pound pkg. baby carrots
6 T. butter
3 T. honey
Salt and pepper to taste
Fresh parsley, for garnish (optional)

Cook and drain carrots; return to saucepan. Over medium heat add butter, add honey, salt and pepper; blend and coat well. Cover and simmer for 5 minutes. Sprinkle with parsley before serving if desired. Serves 4 to 6.

BEAUFORT BAKED ACORN SQUASH

2 acorn squash
1 stick butter
Brown sugar
Salt and pepper

Preheat oven to 350° F. Cut squash in half lengthwise and seed. Place squash cut side down in a large roasting pan; pour in approximately 1/2 inch of water. Cover with foil and bake for 30 minutes. Drain water and turn squash right side up and cut in half lengthwise to form wedges. Prick surface overall with fork; sprinkle with salt and pepper. Spoon 1 tablespoon or more brown sugar in each wedge; spreading it around; top with a generous pat of butter. Cover with foil and bake an additional 30 minutes or more until sugar is melted and squash is fork tender. Serves 4.

BAKED ONIONS

Medium sweet onion, 1 per person
Pepper
Chicken or beef bouillon cubes
Butter

Preheat oven to 350° F. Remove outer shell of onion; place onion on a sheet of foil. Score the onion two-thirds of the way through. Sprinkle with pepper. Place bouillon cube on top of the onion along with a pat of butter. Wrap tightly in foil. Bake for one hour or until onion is tender.

SEASONING FOR VEGETABLES

4 T. bread crumbs
8 T. butter
1/2 tsp. dry mustard
2 T. fresh parsley, chopped
Grated rind of 1 lemon
1 tsp. favorite herb mix

Melt butter in a skillet, add bread crumbs and dry mustard; brown well. Add parsley, lemon rind and herbs. Toss with any green vegetable. Makes 1/2 cup.

CREAMED MUSHROOMS

1 pound fresh mushrooms, sliced
1/4 cup butter
2 T. flour
2 cups milk
1/4 tsp. salt
1-1/2 tsp. Worcestershire

Simmer mushrooms in water for 5 minutes; drain. Melt butter in saucepan. Stir in flour, gradually stir in milk; cook; stirring constantly until slightly thickened and smooth. Stir in salt, Worcestershire and mushrooms. Simmer for an additional 30 minutes, stirring occasionally.

STUFFED POTATOES WITH SHRIMP

4 medium baking potatoes
4 T. butter
1/2 cup milk
1/2 tsp. salt
2 cups shrimp, cooked, peeled and de-veined, cut into bite-sized pieces
1/4 cup mushrooms, sliced
1 cup cheddar cheese, shredded

Bake potatoes in oven for 1 hour at 450° F. Turn temperature to 400° F when potatoes are done. Cut potatoes in half lengthwise; scoop out, being careful not to harm the shells. Mash the potatoes minus the shells; beat in butter, milk and salt. Fold in diced shrimp and mushroom. Pile lightly into shells sprinkle with cheese and bake for 15 minutes or until cheese is melted.

RICE PILAF

1 cup uncooked rice
2- 14 oz. cans chicken stock
1 cup fresh mushrooms, chopped
1 T. green onion tops, sliced

Rinse rice under cold water until water runs clear. Place rice in a 3 quart casserole dish; Add chicken stock, mushrooms and onion. Stir. Bake uncovered at 350° F for 45 minutes to 1 hour, stirring occasionally until all the liquid has been absorbed and the rice is tender.

BACK BAY BISCUITS SUPREME

2 cups flour
1/2 tsp. salt
2 tsp. sugar
4 tsp. baking powder
1/2 tsp. cream of tartar
1/2 cup margarine
2/3 cup milk

Pre-heat oven to 450°F. Sift dry ingredients together. Cut in margarine until mixture resembles coarse crumbs. Add milk all at once; stir just until the dough follows the fork around the bowl. Roll out dough to 1/2" thickness. Cut with biscuit cutter. Place on ungreased cookie sheet. Bake for 10 to 12 minutes.

CHEESY HERB BREAD

Large loaf Italian Bread or crusty bread of choice, unsliced
1 T. Parmesan cheese
1 T. butter
1 tsp. garlic powder
1 tsp. caraway
1 tsp. oregano
1 tsp. parsley

Melt butter and add remaining seasonings; let sit over night. Slice bread but not all the way through—gently spread inside; spread each slice with herb mixture. Sprinkle loaf with parmesan cheese. Wrap loaf with foil. Bake at 400°F for 15 minutes.

SAUTEÉD ALMOND RICE

1/2 cup uncooked rice
1/2 cup sliced almonds
1/2 cup fresh mushrooms, sliced
3 T. butter
1 can onion soup
2/3 cup hot water

In a frying pan, melt butter over medium heat, brown rice. Add almonds and cook until lightly browned. Add mushrooms; cook approximately 10 minutes, stirring frequently. Add soup, water and stir. Bring to boil, reduce heat and cover and cook 25 minutes or until all the liquid has been absorbed and rice is tender. Serves 4.

GARDEN RICE SALAD

1 pkg. seasoned long grain and wild rice mix
1/2 cup mayonnaise
1/4 cup plain yogurt
1 cup tomato, cubed
1/2 cup cucumber, diced
2 tsp. parsley, chopped
1/8 tsp. salt
1/8 tsp. pepper

Cook rice according to directions. Cool. Stir remaining ingredients together in a large bowl. Add rice; toss gently; cover and chill. Best served cold. Serves 4.

RED CABBAGE AND BEETS

1 small onion, sliced
2 T. butter
4 cups red cabbage, finely shredded
3 medium beets
3/4 cup water
3 T. vinegar
1 cup beef broth
1 tsp. salt
1/8 tsp. pepper

Parboil, peel and shred beets; set aside. Melt butter over medium heat in a large frying pan; sauté onion until lightly browned. Add remaining ingredients and bring to a boil. Cover and cook 10 to 15 minutes or until tender. Serves 6 to 8.

HERBED CHEESE SPREAD

4 oz. sharp cheddar cheese, shredded
2 T. heavy cream
3 T. dry sherry
1/2 tsp. salt
1/2 tsp. chives, minced
1/8 tsp. white pepper
1/8 tsp. ground sage
1/8 tsp. tarragon leaves
1/8 tsp. dried thyme leaves
1/4 tsp. dry mustard

Combine all ingredients in a double boiler. Heat over hot water stirring constantly until cheese melts and mixture is smooth. Pour into 2 small custard cups or into decorative crocks and chill. Serve cheese at room temperature with assorted crackers. Best made 1 or 2 days ahead to allow flavors to blend.

CANADIAN HOLE ZUCCHINI AND STEWED TOMATOES

6 medium zucchini, approximately 8" long
1 large sweet onion
4 stalks celery
1 can stewed tomatoes
2 tsp. salt
1/4 cup sugar
Parmesan cheese

This recipe requires a large saucepan or a Dutch oven. Peel zucchini; cut into large chunks; place in pan. Cut onion into large chunks and add to zucchini. Cut celery in 1/2" diagonal pieces; add to pan. Add the salt, sugar and stewed tomatoes with the juice. Cover and bring to a boil. Reduce heat and cook until zucchini is tender. Serve in individual bowls. Sprinkle individual servings with Parmesan cheese.

DESSERTS

Situated near the Cape Fear River and the Atlantic Ocean, Oak Island Lighthouse came into service in 1958 after replacing Bald Head Island Lighthouse. Designed to warn mariners of the dangerous Frying Pan Shoals, this black, white and gray banded lighthouse is 169 feet tall and is visible for 19 miles. Built upon a bed of solid rock, the Oak Island Lighthouse can sway as much as three feet in 60 mph winds.

SWEET KITTY CAKE

1 cup oil
2 cups sugar
3 eggs
1 tsp. salt
1 tsp. baking soda
1 tsp. cinnamon
2 cups flour
2 cups bananas, diced
8 oz. can crushed pineapple

Cream Cheese Frosting:

3 oz. cream cheese, softened
1/4 cup butter, softened
1 cup powdered sugar
1 tsp. vanilla

Preheat oven to 350° F. Grease and flour a 9"x13" baking pan. Sift flour, salt, baking soda and cinnamon together; set aside. Mix oil, sugar and eggs in a large mixing bowl; add flour; mix well. Gently fold in bananas and pineapple. Pour into prepared baking pan. Bake 45 to 50 minutes. Cool cake completely before frosting.

Cream cheese frosting:

Cream butter and cream cheese together in a large bowl; add powdered sugar in a little at a time. Add vanilla and blend well.

LOREN'S LEMON SQUARES

1/2 cup butter
1/2 cup solid margarine
2 cups sugar
4 eggs, beaten
1/3 cup fresh lemon juice
1/2 cup powdered sugar
1/2 tsp. baking powder
1/2 cup flour
2 cups sifted flour

Preheat oven to 350° F. Sift together 2 cups of flour and powdered sugar in a large bowl. Cut butter and margarine into flour mixture until mixture clings together. Press dough mixture into an ungreased 9"x13"baking pan. Bake for 20 minutes or until lightly browned. Mix sugar and lemon juice together, add 1/2 cup of flour and baking powder and combine with beaten eggs. Pour over baked crust and bake for 25 minutes. Sprinkle with powdered sugar when cooled.

DARBY'S CHOCOLATE MACAROONS

2 cups sugar
1 stick butter
1/2 cup milk
3 T. cocoa
3 cups rolled oats
1/2 cup crunchy peanut butter
1 tsp. vanilla

In a saucepan over medium heat combine sugar, butter, milk and cocoa; bring to a boil. Boil for one minute then remove from heat. Add oats, peanut butter and vanilla; blend well. Drop by teaspoonfuls on waxed paper.

PIRATE PLEASIN' PEANUT BUTTER OATMEAL COOKIES

3/4 cup butter
1/2 cup peanut butter
1 cup sugar
1 cup brown sugar, firmly packed
2 eggs
1/4 cup milk
1 tsp. vanilla
1 tsp. baking soda
1 tsp. salt
1 tsp. cinnamon
2 cups sifted flour
1-1/2 cups quick oats
1 cup raisins

Preheat oven 350° F. Sift flour, cinnamon, salt and baking soda together; set aside. In a large mixing bowl, cream butter and peanut butter together; add brown and white sugars and eggs; mix well. Add milk, vanilla and flour. When all ingredients are well incorporated, add oats and raisins. Drop by tablespoonfuls on greased cookie sheet. Bake for 15 minutes or until golden brown.

BUCKEYE CANDY

1-1/2 cups creamy peanut butter
1 pound powdered sugar
1 stick butter, softened
1 tsp. vanilla
1 pound milk chocolate discs for melting

Cream peanut butter, sugar, butter and vanilla together and roll into 1" diameter balls. Melt half the chocolate at a time in a microwave or over a double boiler. Insert a toothpick approximately half way into the peanut butter ball and carefully dip into the melted chocolate to coat 3/4 of the way up—do not coat entirely. Place on waxed paper until set.

BREAD PUDDING

8 slices day-old white bread
1/2 stick butter, softened
5 eggs
2-1/4 cups of milk
1/2 cup sugar
1 tsp. cinnamon, combined with 1/4 cup sugar
1 tsp. vanilla
1/2 cup raisins

Preheat oven to 350°. Grease a 9" square baking dish. In a small mixing bowl or a shaker, mix cinnamon and 1/4 cup of sugar; set aside. Butter one side of each slice of bread. Place 4 slices in the bottom of baking dish; sprinkle generously with cinnamon mixture and cover with raisins. Place another layer of buttered bread with cinnamon sugar on top. In a separate bowl, beat eggs, milk, sugar, and vanilla, stirring until the sugar is dissolved. Slowly pour over bread mixture and allow the liquid to be absorbed by the bread. Place the baking dish in a 9"x13" baking pan with 1 inch of hot water. The water will keep it from burning on the bottom. Bake for 60 minutes, or until a knife blade inserted 1/2 inch comes out clean. Serve warm or chilled.

BANANA BOATS

Bananas
Miniature marshmallows
Milk chocolate candy bars broken into squares

Preheat oven to 350° F. Peel only one strip of banana peel down to the end of the banana, being careful not to remove it all the way off the banana. With a teaspoon, scoop out a trough about the width of your thumb the full length of the banana. Alternate stuffing the entire length of the trough with a miniature marsh-mallow followed by a square of milk chocolate. Replace the banana peel over the trough, wrap in foil and place in 350° F oven for 15 minutes or on a bed of hot coals at a campfire.

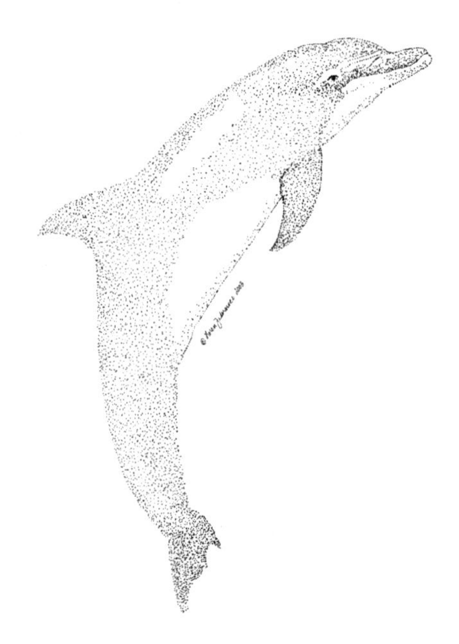

Dolphins are air breathing mammals that live in the sea. Living in groups called pods, the Bottlenose Dolphins are the most popular of all dolphins because of their friendliness toward humans. The Bottlenose Dolphin acquired its name because of the shape of its beak; it reminded people of old-fashion bottles. Dolphins feed on a wide variety of fish, including squid.

MINI CUPCAKES

8 oz. pkg. softened cream cheese
1 egg
1/3 cup sugar
12 oz. pkg. chocolate chips
1-1/2 cups flour
1 cup sugar
1/2 cup cocoa
1 tsp. baking soda
1/2 tsp. salt
1 cup water
1/3 cup oil
1 tsp. vanilla

Preheat oven to 350° F. Mix cream cheese, 1/3 cup sugar and dash of salt together. Add egg and mix well. Fold in chocolate chips and set aside. In a separate bowl, combine flour, 1 cup sugar, cocoa, baking soda and salt. Add oil, water and vanilla and mix well. Use mini cupcake pans and liners. Fill each liner 1/3 cup full with chocolate mixture and top with less than 1 teaspoonful of cream cheese mixture. Bake at 350° F for 20 minutes. These freeze well. *Helpful hint:* Pour the chocolate batter into a 2 cup measuring cup to pour it into cupcake liners.

CRUMB CAKE

2-1/2 cups flour
2 cups brown sugar
1/2 cup shortening
2 tsp. baking powder
1 tsp. baking soda
1 cup sour cream
2 eggs
1 tsp. vanilla
Cinnamon

Preheat oven to 350° F. Mix brown sugar, flour, shortening, baking powder and baking soda. Reserve 1 cup of mixture for crumb topping. Add remaining ingredients and pour batter into a greased 9"x13" baking pan. Sprinkle the reserved crumbs on top and bake at 350° F for 30 minutes. Lightly dust cinnamon over the top of the cake before baking or when it comes out of the oven.

SOFT SUGAR COOKIES

1 cup shortening
1-1/2 cup sugar
2 eggs, beaten
1/2 tsp. baking soda
1 tsp. baking powder
1/2 tsp. salt
3 cups flour
3/4 cup sour cream
1 tsp. vanilla

Preheat oven to 350° F. Sift flour, salt, baking powder, and baking soda together; set aside. Cream shortening and sugar together; add eggs. When well mixed, add sour cream and vanilla. Add flour mixture and blend well. Drop by teaspoonfuls on to an ungreased cookie sheet and sprinkle with sugar. Bake at 350° F for 8 to 10 minutes.

SOFT AND LIGHT CHOCOLATE CHIP COOKIES

1 cup shortening
1 cup white sugar
1 cup brown sugar, firmly packed
2 eggs
1 cup sour cream
1 tsp. baking soda
1/2 tsp. salt
1/2 tsp. vanilla
4-1/2 cups flour
1 cup nuts (optional)
1 - 12oz. pkg. chocolate chips

Preheat oven to 350° F. In a large bowl, or a heavy duty mixer, cream together shortening, white sugar, and brown sugar. Add eggs, sour cream, baking soda, salt, and vanilla. Slowly add flour, mixing well. Add nuts and chocolate chips. Drop by teaspoonfuls on to an ungreased cookie sheet. Bake at 350° F for 8 to 10 minutes.

CANDY'S BEST PIE CRUST EVER

3 cups flour
1/2 cup butter, softened
1 tsp. salt
1 tsp. sugar
1 cup of Crisco
3 T. cold water
1 egg
1 T. vinegar

Cut butter and Crisco into dry ingredients until dough is pea-sized; continue until dough resembles corn meal. In a separate bowl, beat egg, vinegar, and water until well blended; add to flour mixture with fork. Do not overwork the piecrust dough. This dough is meant to be very wet. Roll out between 2 sheets of waxed paper. Makes three 9" pie crusts.

CANDY'S PEACH COBBLER PIE

1-1/2 cups sugar
1/2 cup flour
1/3 cup butter
1 tsp. vanilla
1 egg, beaten
sliced peaches

Preheat oven to 400° F. Cream first four ingredients together, add egg and mix well. Spread over fresh, peeled, sliced peaches and place into 9" unbaked pie crust. Place pie on a cookie sheet in center of the oven. Bake at 400° F for 10 minutes, then lower the temperature to 350° F and bake an additional 50 minutes.

TWO TONE CHEESE CAKE

Graham cracker crust

2 - 8 oz. pkg. cream cheese
3 eggs
1/2 cup sugar
1 tsp. vanilla

Topping

1 pint sour cream
1/2 cup sugar
1 tsp. vanilla

Preheat oven to 375° F. Prepare a graham cracker crust to fit a 9"x13" baking pan. In a large mixing bowl, blend cream cheese, eggs, sugar and vanilla; pour over graham cracker crust. Bake for 20 minutes. Cool to room temperature.

Topping: Mix sour cream, sugar and vanilla and pour over cooled cheese. Place back in the oven. Bake at 475° F for 10 minutes. Cool. Chill before serving.

RASPBERRY COFFEE CAKE

3 oz. cream cheese
1/4 cup butter
2 cups biscuit mix
1/3 cup milk
1/2 cup raspberry preserves
Powdered sugar

Preheat oven to 425°F. Cut cream cheese and butter into biscuit mix until crumbly; add milk and mix. Turn dough out on to a lightly floured surface; knead 8 to 10 times. Roll out into a 12"x18" rectangle and place on a greased baking sheet. Spread raspberry preserves down center of dough. Fold one side of the dough over the filling followed by folding the remaining side over the middle. Cut 2 1/2" long slits in 1" increments, across the top and down the entire length of dough. Bake for 12 to 15 minutes. Sprinkle with powdered sugar.

TEXAS SHEET CAKE

2 sticks of margarine
1 cup water
4 T. cocoa
2 cups flour
2 cups sugar
1/2 tsp. salt
2 eggs
1/2 cup sour cream
1 tsp. baking soda

Preheat oven to 375° F. In a saucepan, combine margarine, water and cocoa; bring to a boil. Remove from heat and add flour, sugar and salt; beat in eggs, sour cream and baking soda. Pour into a jelly roll pan or a cookie sheet with sides. Bake at 375°F for 22 minutes. Remove cake from oven and let cool for 5 minutes or less. Ice cake while still warm.

Icing:

1 stick margarine
4 T. cocoa
6 T. milk
1 pound of powdered sugar
1 tsp. vanilla
1 cup chopped nuts (optional)

In a saucepan, bring margarine, cocoa and milk to a boil. Remove from heat and using an electric mixer add 1 pound of powdered sugar, 1 teaspoon vanilla and beat until smooth. Mix in 1 cup chopped nuts and spread over warm cake.

APPLE CRISP

1 stick margarine, room temperature
1 cup brown sugar, packed firm
1 cup flour
1 cup rolled oats, not quick oats
1 T. cinnamon
1/2 cup white sugar
1/2 stick butter
8 large apples or enough to fill a 9"x13" baking pan

Preheat oven to 375° F. Peel and slice apples; place in a 9"x13" baking pan. Sprinkle 1/2 cup sugar over apples and dot with pats of butter.

Crumb topping: In a large mixing bowl, combine flour, brown sugar and cinnamon; add margarine. Cut margarine into the flour and sugar to resemble coarse crumbs. Add oatmeal; mix by cutting the oatmeal into the mixture to keep it crumbly. Spoon a heavy layer of crumb topping over the entire pan of apples. Bake for approximately 45 minutes or until apples are tender and topping is lightly browned.

INDEX